LOVE SONGS OF KABIR

Love Songs of *Kabir*

G. N. Das

Foreword by
K. S. Duggal

Abhinav Publications

HIND POCKET BOOKS

LOVE SONGS OF KABIR
© G. N. Das
First published in Hardcover by Abhinav Publications, New Delhi.
First published in Paperback in 2012 by Hind Pocket Books
under arrangement with Abhinav Publications.

ISBN 978-81-216-1769-7

All rights reserved. No part of this book may be reproduced or transmitted in any form or by any means, electronic, mechanical including photocopying, recording or by any storage and retrieval system, without permission in writing from the publishers.

Publisher
Shakti Malik
Abhinav Publications,
E-37, Hauz Khas, New Delhi-110016

This edition exclusively distributed throughout the world by
Hind Pocket Books Pvt. Ltd.
E-14, Sector-11, Noida-201301
Tel: +0120 4162707, 4163707
E-mail: sales@hindpocketbooks.in • website: www.hindpocketbooks.in

Printed at Star Printo Bind, New Delhi-110020
PRINTED IN INDIA

DEDICATION

This little work of translation of one hundred and one of the captivating love songs of Kabir is humbly dedicated to the celebrated scholar and writer on Sant Kabir, late Padmashree Dr. Ram Kumar Verma, but for whose inspiring encouragement I would not have been able to do it.

LOVE SONGS OF KABIR

(Being translation in free verse of one hundred and one songs of Kabir portraying the *prema lilaa* (love game) between the *jivathmaa* (soul of man) and *paramathmaa* (Supreme Soul or God)

> The lock of error shuts the door
> of the mansion of your Love.
> Use the key of love and open
> the door and windows too,
> and thus wake up your Love.
> Says Kabir O, gentle folk listen!
> you cannot get this chance again.
>
> —*Kabir*

CONTENTS

Foreword	9
Preface	13
Acknowledgements	26
Appreciation	27
Message	29
Introduction	31
Diacriticals	37
Text	39
Glossary	171
Bibliography	176
Index of first lines of the songs (English translation) included in the book	177

FOREWORD

Born 600 years ago and said to have lived for 129 years (1389-1518 A.D.), Kabir belonged to Bhakti Movement with a marked strain of mysticism. It was the time when the Moghuls and Afghans had decided that rather than plundering and returning, they would occupy what they called Hindustan and settle here for good. In order that a reasonable equation was brought about between the two religious communities, the Sufis and Bhaktas started striving for it. A disciple of Ramanand, Kabir is believed to have made significant contribution towards this cause.

Maybe, Kabir was specifically commissioned for the task. There is an interesting anecdote about his birth. It is said that there lived a Brahmin at Varanasi who was a devotee of Ramanand. The Brahmin had a daughter who was a virgin-widow. She longed to pay homage to Ramanand. Her father, one day, took the girl along with him. As she prostrated before Ramanand and touched his feet, the master blessed her with a son. Considering that the girl was a virgin-widow, the Brahmin was in a queer predicament. Ramanand's words, however, could not be recalled. In due course, the girl gave birth to a son whom they surreptitiously abandoned by the side of a lake, a little distance away from the town. Soon thereafter the baby was spotted by a Muslim weaver and his wife who, as it happened, were issueless. They adopted the child and named him Kabir.

Born of a Brahmin mother and brought up in a Muslim family, Kabir was, as it were, made for bringing about understanding and amity between the Hindus and Muslims of his time.

He was a no nonsense godman. He rejected ritualism and the unnecessary ceremonials prevalent amongst both the Hindus and Muslims. His approach towards religion was essentially rational. He wanted the Hindus to be good Hindus and the Muslims to be good Muslims. He condemned the curse of caste system and its no uncertain impact on Islam in India, vehemently. For him Ram and Rahim were the same. He believed that there was no such thing as high caste and low caste. All men are born equal. He challenged the Brahmin of his day—'If you are Brahmin, born of a Brahmin mother, why did you not take birth by a different course? How come, I am blood and you are milk?'

He found fault with idol-worship of the Hindus. He admonished the devotee telling him that every leaf that he plucked for his offering had life in it while the idol he worshipped was lifeless. Says Kabir:

> If God can be had by worshipping a stone,
> I'll worship a mountain.
> Better than the stone idol is a handmill
> That grinds corn, the man to sustain.

Similarly, he was critical of the Muslim way of life, not sparing even some of the provisions of the Islamic Shariat. He insisted on clean living making no difference between a devout Hindu and a Godfearing Muslim. Says Kabir:

> Make your mind the Kaaba, your body its enclosure,
> And your conscience the teacher.
> O Mulla, then only call people for prayer in the mosque
> That has ten gates.

No wonder that he alienated both the Hindus and Muslims who made a complaint against him to the king. Kabir was summoned to the court. During the course of argument it was discovered, what to speak of Islam and Brahminism, Kabir seemed to find fault even with God:

> O God, you must decide an issue
> If you wish this slave to serve you.
> Is the soul or to whom it is devoted the greater?
> Is God or he who knows Him the greater?
> Is Brahmin or who created him the greater?
> Is the pilgrimage or the pilgrim the greater?
> Says Kabir, this is my predicament.

There came a stage in his life when Kabir withdrew himself from the worldly duties altogether and devoted himself exclusively to the spiritual pursuits. This led to unpleasantness. A family man, quitting his profession and taking to what his people considered ungainful pursuits! An evolved soul, Kabir paid no heed to his sorrowing mother. He has recorded this in one of his hymns:

> Kabir's mother sobs and screams.
> How is he going to maintain his family, O Lord?
> He has given up his weaving
> And taken to repeating God's name.
> Says Kabir, as the thread passes through the spool
> It makes me forget my beloved God for a moment.
> I am mean, a weaver that I am!
> God's name is the gift I have gained.

Listen my mother,
God will provide for us all.

The Sufis of his time believed that one way to attain God (Ishq Haquiqi) was through worldly love (Ishq Majazi). You love the physical person of your beloved so intensely that a stage comes when the worldly love sublimates itself into spiritual love. That Kabir subscribed to it is evident from his verse. He composed a large number of love-songs that are marked for their sensuous overtones:

> My eyes are heavy with sleep my love,
> Come, let us go to bed.
> Lovelorn, my body quivers and quakes.
>
> x x x   x x x
>
> The flowers I decked my bed with
> Are drooping and dying fast.
> Do step cautiously on the bed, my love!
> My sister and my aunt are still awake. (L.S. No.43)

It is the intense longing of the devotee that qualifies him to attain enlightenment. It is one-pointed search. It entails a great deal of sacrifice. It is constant day and night pursuit. And when the devotee arrives, he must not relax. He must entrench the Lord to his heart:

> In dream did my Love come to me.
> I woke up at His tender touch.
> In order to retain the bliss of my dream
> I do not at all open my eyes.   (L.S. No.5)

The path is arduous. It is beset with not a few hazards. Man is inherently prone to the five vices—lust, avarice, ire, attachment, and ego. They are like predators, the Bedouines in the pilgrims way to Mecca. One must guard against them:

> Reckless runs the crooked stream of longings,
> None can curb its flow.
> Lust and ire two enemies dire
> Plunge one in the sea of worldly vice.   (L.S. No. 7)

However, if God so pleases, one can be saved. The Bhakti Movement laid stress on Grace. No amount of man's effort avails. He must evoke the Divine pleasure. The Guru shows the way and it is God's grace that gets to the goal:

> Says Kabir—O, friends know it for certain
> Without the kind Guru's grace
> None can hope to win His love. (L.S.No. 60)

The Divine bliss is enchanting. It is like nothing else known to the mortal being:

> Full moon shines there every night
> Every day is sunny and bright
> With myriad suns' effulgence. (L.S.No. 9)

x x x x x x

> Where sweet music swells from the flute
> And lotus blooms all the year round. (L.S.No. 17)

It is not easy attaining the Divine love. It asks for heavy price, at times even the head of the seeker:

> Love does not grow in field and forest,
> Nor is it sold in shop and market.
> Rich or poor, you can have it
> If you sever your head
> And lay it at His feet. (L.S.No. 16)

A great saint and social reformer, Kabir was not only the forerunner of the Bhakti Movement, he is, probably, the most sensitive and perceptive poet of his time. The thought-content, the diction and the liquid lyricism of this hymn in the original will do credit to any poet of his age:

> A fine texture I have woven this fabric.
> It was woven by sages and saints.
> They wore it and dirtied it.
> Kabir the humble, wore it with such care;
> It remained as it was when he took it off.

The mystic in the poet takes pride in it, the Bhakta in him remains the humble Kabir.

Shri Gananath's translation of Kabir's love songs into free verse is laudable indeed, more especially in the year of the saint-poet's Sixth Birth Centenary. The devotion with which he has gone about his job is creditable.

P-7, Hauz Khas Enclave　　　　　　　　　　　K.S. Duggal
New Delhi-110016　　　　　　　　　　　　　　12.3.89

PREFACE

Kabir (1389-1518 A.D.) was endowed from birth with deep spiritual insight and strong common sense combined with deep sympathy and love for his fellow beings. He enriched this by taking lessons from the book of life and watching intently the social, political and spiritual scene around him.

As he grew up he spurned the idea of going in for formal education for he considered it enough to learn only the two letters which make Rama, his Eternal Supreme God, rather than all the fifty-two alphabets. And, he showed its validity in his own life.

With the guidance of the then eminent spiritual leader Ramanand, whom he got as his preceptor, and extensive contact and communion with seers and saints of various faiths like Hinduism with its numerous sects such as Baishnab, Saiva, Ganapatya, Shakta etc, Islam, Sufism, Hatha Yogis, Nathpanthis, Buddhism, Jainism and so on which existed side by side occasionally jostling one another, and Kabir drew his own lessons from each of them and on their reactions to one another.

As Kabir advanced in his spiritual development he gained the deep rooted conviction that man was created by God in his own image, the soul in man *(Jivathma)* being part and parcel of the Supreme Soul *(Paramathma)*. This idea he accepted from Hindu philosophy. And, though each of the two viz *Jivathma* and *Paramathma* is ever eager to unite with the other it depended on the man *(Jiva)* concerned how far he was able to help or hinder this process. If he would lead a noble and clean life it would be helpful for his soul to achieve the goal of union or else if he indulged in evil deeds it would impede the process by exerting adverse influence on the efforts of his soul.

It is, therefore, of utmost importance, Kabir held, that man should follow the right path in life in his thought, word and deed and remain steadfast in his devotion to *Paramathma*. This will facilitate his soul to come close and closer to *Paramathma* till at length the soul in him unites with the Supreme Soul.

The whole process of the soul and the Supreme Soul heading towards each other and their final union has been termed as *lila* or spiritual love game and their ultimate union as spiritual marriage by spiritual leaders, seers and saints, particularly of the *Rahasyabad* or mystic schools of thought.

Scholars, spiritual leaders, and seers have racked their brain and gone into intensive enquiry as to why God *(Paramathma)* being Himself Almighty should have thought of such a process as *Lila* to effect the union of *Jivathma* and *Paramathma* (Himself). They have not found the answer to that and have remained satisfied holding that *lila* is for *lila* sake only. There cannot be any explanation for it.

In the view of Kabir love is the basic ingredient of devotion to the Lord. For Kabir without love devotion is meaningless:

> Devotion without love of the Lord
> > If held as devotion
> You do so out of insolence
> > Wasting your life anon.

(Kabir Doha)

According to Kabir love plays the most vital part in the union of soul and Supreme Soul. The following lines of Sl. 89 make that self evident:

> If my love could reach Him
> The heat of my body and mind would vanish
> Says Kabir—if I too could get His love
> I would join my face with His
> and drink from the same cup of love with Him.

(L.S. 89)

It is said that Kabir drew upon the *Sufi* view that the attraction between *jivathma* and *paramathma* towards each other is based on love for their ultimate union. According to the Sufis *jivathma* (human soul) which should be the prime mover in this game of love between the two is to be taken as the masculine element because they hold that the love of the man for the woman is always stronger and more eloquent than that of the woman for the man.

Kabir, however, preferred to accept the Baishnab view that the love of the woman is always stronger and more ardent and, therefore, *Jivathma* which has to be the prime mover must represent the feminine element in the game between the two. *Paramathma* being the only masculine element (*Parama Purusha*) will be sought after ardently by the feminine element for the Union.

In hundreds of his love songs portraying the *Prema Lila* (game of love) between the *Jivathma* and *Paramathma* Kabir has taken the former as the feminine and the latter as the masculine element.

In these songs, one hundred and one of which follow, the saint-poet has in a poignant manner in his homely diction and similes portrayed the urge of love and the pang of separation that the *Jivathma* feels and suffers for want of her Love (*Paramathma*) and also the efforts she makes and hopes and fears she entertains in her heart.

At times *Jivathma* harbours the fear that she has neither

personal charm and beauty nor deep enough love and devotion for her love to be able to win Him:

> Deep and strong is not my love
> Nor have I a beauteous face
> I know not how I can gain
> My Beloved's love and grace.
>
> (Kabir Doha)

In Sl. 15 of these songs Kabir gives vent to the same sense of uncertainty and doubt:

> I do not know what my Love will do
> so I am quaking in constant fear

xxx xxx xxx

Sometimes *Jivathma* is confident that her Love is coming to woo and wed her:

> Today will my Love come to my house
> I am washing my courtyard again and again
> bedecked I am with gems and gold.

xxx xxx xxx

> Says Kabir—What luck
> tonight I shall wed the Supreme Lord! (L.S. 34)

At times the *Jivathma* fancies her Love has already come to her hut and she is going to wed Him and sings:

> Young bride
> do sing the welcome song
> my Love has come to my hut today

xxx xxx xxx

> Says Kabir—O my luck
> I am going to wed my dear Love
> the Lord Supreme.   (L.S. 1)

Time and again she gives vent to her deep agony for want of her Love. For instance,

> Intense is my agony
> for want of my Love

I am passing my days in great distress
and nights without a wink of sleep.   (L.S. 3)

       xxx   xxx   xxx

How deep and intense is the *jivathma's* love for Him:

In dream did my Love come to me
I woke up to His tender touch.
To retain the bliss of my dream
I do not at all open my eyes.
Do come once inside my eye my Love
I shall at once drop the lids
So I alone shall see You there
and none else You can see!   (L.S. 5)

In more poignant words Kabir has given vent to the yearning of the *Jivathma* for union with *Paramathma* in the following manner:

       xxx   xxx   xxx

I shall draw from the gathering clouds
the stream of tears to my eyes
and with their lowering dark shadow
cover up my heart.
I shall bring my face close to His
and whisper in His ears
the yearning of my heart.

       xxx   xxx   xxx

(L.S. 87)

At times *Jivathma* wants to gain her Love by winning a game of dice on wager played with Him:

I have staked my body and mind
to play dice on wager with my Love.
If I lose my Love wins me
if I win He becomes mine.

       xxx   xxx   xxx

In the game of dice
this dual hope is always there.   (L.S. 71)

The hundred and one songs that follow depict in Kabir's

inimitable style and diction and with a rich store of homely similes the longing of the *Jivathma* for uniting with *Paramathma*. Almost each is a fresh exposition of the *Jivatma's* endless effort to gain her point.

In Kabir's view the *Jiva* (man) concerned can hope for the success of his *athma* (soul) provided his urge for Him *(Paramathma)* is true and deep like that of the chaste wife for her husband. If not all his efforts go in vain:

> I shivered in fear and shame
> and wondered how
> I can unite with my Love
> if I have not shed my bashfulness
> uncovered my face, made body bare
> and clasped and clung to my Love
> and in the light of my eyes
> glanced his charming winsome face
> says Kabir—O my friends listen
> she alone can comprehend
> if her love for Him is true and deep
> but if not so
> futile will be all her make up.   (L.S. 39)

And, Kabir held that in order to develop true and deep love for God *(Paramathma)* one has to cleanse his mind and heart which is the seat of God *(Paramathma)* in the form of his soul. For achieving that one has to follow the right path of duty in thought, word, and deed. Unless man controls his mind, abandons pride, anger, lust, greed and attachment he will easily fall prey to evil forces both inside and outside him and thereby lose the chance of helping his soul to unite with the Supreme Soul. Not only that, he will slide down in the birth-death cycle and take many many births before he can hope to be reborn as a human and get the chance again for his salvation.

In Sl. 71 the above is clearly foreshadowed in the following words:

xxx   xxx   xxx

> Moving from square to square
> if I cannot play the dice correctly
> at the crucial stage
> I shall fail to enter the home square
> and reach the Lord.

And I slide back again
to repeat moving from square to square.

xxx   xxx   xxx

In the view of all religions the ultimate goal of man is to attain salvation or union of *atma* or the soul in him with the Supreme Soul *(Paramathma)*. In Sl. 10 Kabir clearly indicates that humans draw their origin from the Heavenly father *(Paramathma)* and must go back there on attaining salvation:

O my mind!
You do not yet know the City of Your Love
just as you have come from there
so you shall go back.

xxx   xxx   xxx

Look my Love is waiting on the other shore
You pay no heed to that meeting!

xxx   xxx   xxx

This concept of Hindu philosophy has also been echoed by the eighteenth century poet laureate of England, William Wordsworth, who in his well known poem "Ode on intimations of immortality" gives expression to it in the following words:

xxx   xxx   xxx

Our birth is but a sleep and forgetting
The soul that rises with us, our life's star
Hath had elsewhere its setting
And cometh from afar
Not in entire forgetfulness
Not in utter nakedness
But trailing clouds of glory do we come
From God who is our home.

xxx   xxx   xxx

Heaven lies about us in our infancy
Shades of the prison house begin to close
Upon the growing Boy.

xxx   xxx   xxx

Earth fills her lap with pleasure of her own
yearnings she hath in her natural kind

> And even with something of a mother's mind
> And no unworthy aim
> The homely nurse doth all she can
> To make her foster child her inmate, Man
> Forget the glories he hath known
> And that imperial palace whence he came.

xxx   xxx   xxx

Kabir is referring to this "imperial palace" of God when he is talking of the city of Love (vide L.S. 10).

Kabir has also spoken in the same vein more specifically in the following words:

> Long long ago my soul parted
> from my Lord the Soul Supreme
> and now she craves reunion
> but being unable is suffering
> the severe pang of separation.   (L.S. 78)

xxx   xxx   xxx

> Says Kabir—O Lord long long since
> I parted from You.
> Now my mind is too restless
> for the reunion
> do extend Your kind hand
> and take me near You
> my Lord do hear my entreaty.   (L.S. 80)

In a couple of his dohas Kabir touchingly describes how the human soul unites and mingles in the Supreme Soul:

> Says Kabir, soul craves Supreme Soul
>   To lose itself in Him
> Love-lorn the soul nears the goal
>   Quivering mingles in the Beam.

and

> On return soul mingles in Supreme Soul
>   In heavenly effulgence
> Where master and servant do mingle
>   Eternal spring prevails.

Although according to Kabir following the Baishnab view it is the *Jivathma* who has to take the initiative in the *Prema Lila* (Love game) with *Paramathma,* the latter is not altogether passive. We may notice from the following examples in the love songs included here that *Paramathma* is also interested in the game and is taking initiative or helping the *Jivathma* to perform her part in it.

> I was deep asleep in my cottage
> Your words of love
> struck my ear and woke me up.
>
> xxx   xxx   xxx
>
> Says Kabir—O gentle soul listen
> my love embraced me in a hug
> and linked my little heart to His. (L.S. 18)
>
> My Love has brought the funeral *sari*
> O my friends it is time for me
> to bid the last adieu.
>
> xxx   xxx   xxx
>
> At the river side the stretcher was lowered
> my Love bent over me
> and smiling tenderly
> lifted the *sari* from my face
> I quaked in the urge of love and fear
> None else was near there
> my Love smiled again
> and picked me up in a tender hug! (L.S. 56)

and also

> I was in deep slumber
> when my Love woke me up,
> I collected the dust of His feet
> and put it in my eyes as *anjan.*
>
> xxx   xxx   xxx
>
> Says Kabir—now the King of death
> is dreading my very sight. (L.S. 80)

If the love songs of Kabir are taken as mere tokens of his mysticism it will be less than what they actually stand for. Sentiments expressed in the songs appear to be real and true as broad day light. Kabir wants in these songs to convey that we hail from God, our Heavenly father, and we shall be failing in our duty if we miss the opportunity to attain our salvation by true love-devotion to Him.

And as he has indicated in many of his songs and dohas (couplets) cleaning up the heart and mind is essential to developing deep sense of love-devotion and self surrender to the Lord. Cleaning up and making the mind and heart pure and as simple as that of the child are in Kabir's view even more rewarding than love-devotion to the Lord. In the following couplet this is quite apparent:

> Says Kabir I have cleansed my mind
> > Pure as Ganges water
> The Lord now runs after me I find
> > calling 'Kabir', 'Kabir'.

and in Sl. 101 of the songs following this has also been indicated in a symbolic manner:

> Standing at the pool
> full of the Lord's Nectar
> the swan is going thirsty!
> She does not know how to drink the Nectar
> without the know-how
> none can drink it my dear!

> > xxx   xxx   xxx

> Says Kabir—my Guru gave me the clue
> following simple innocent habits of moral conduct
> I can realise my Lord Rama.   (L.S. 101)

In one of his other songs (not a love song) Kabir has indicated more specifically how to get the Lord by following a simple moral code of conduct:

> In my effort to get the Lord
> if ever I missed the track
> my Guru showed me the right one.

> > xxx   xxx   xxx

> I offer no *Puja* to the temple deities
> nor do I present flowers to them
> and ring their bells
> I have not become an ascetic
> nor do I burn the sacred fire.
> I obey the moral code of law,
> kind I am to one and all

> and I love all my fellow-beings
> each one is like me in my eyes.
> I have no dispute with any one
> harsh words do not hurt me at all
> pride and greed I have banished from heart.
> Says Kabir—I have no doubt in my mind
> that I shall get the Lord Supreme.

By following the simple rules of moral conduct, becoming pure in mind and heart like a child, surrendering oneself to the Lord, Kabir believes man will attain the objective of salvation and his soul will be in a position to unite with the Supreme Soul in culmination of the *Prema Lila* between them.

Before concluding it would be worthwhile to mention that in certain quarters readers interested in Kabir harbour the feeling that the saint-poet being of a terse temperament bordering on harshness and rather uncompromising in nature for holding on to moral principles in life, it is difficult to comprehend how he could bring himself to write poems depicting intimate love relationship between man and woman be it in the field of spiritual love culminating in marriage or union of the human soul and the Supreme Soul.

It may be true that Kabir had a hard and uncompromising exterior and never minced matters and was never afraid of calling a spade a spade. But, as his couplets and songs reveal he did have a benevolent and not at all a malevolent bent of mind. For instance, the following couplet shows how solicitous he was of the welfare of all his fellow beings:

> Standing in the open market
> Says Kabir—I crave good of all
> With none am I intimate
> And to none inimical.

His harshness was probably due to his dislike of the tardiness of his fellowmen to respond to his call to purify their mind and heart and to surrender to God in love-devotion.

As mentioned earlier Kabir has held categorically that devotion to the Lord without love cannot be called devotion at all. The urge of the soul and the Supreme Soul to come together is based on love for each other. The humal soul is, according to him, a part and parcel of the Supreme Soul and as it is but natural the part will always hanker to unite and blend with the whole.

In Sl. 91 of the songs here included the human soul is seen to be restless for the reunion but finds all the routes to the Supreme

Soul blocked by hurdles which are impeding the effort of the soul. The hurdles are the enemies in the man himself which sully his character and stand in the way of his soul to gain access to the Supreme Soul. In order to overcome the enemies he was advised to follow the paths of knowledge, devotion and self denial. But ultimately it is realised that these will not help him for, says Kabir:

> None can enter the lanes nor emerge
> who does not know the way of love.

In another song (Sl. 13) Kabir has expressed in more specific terms the supremacy of the path of love over the path of knowledge for the *Jivathma* to unite with *Paramathma*.

In the following lines of this song Kabir says symbolically that due to carelessness and ignorance the aspirant (*jiva*) sustains stains on herself which impede the process of union. Her spouse helps her with the soap of knowledge but however diligently she uses it the stains do not go. Concluding Kabir says—the stains will go only when her Love (*Paramathma*) makes her (*Jivathma*) His own i.e. showers His blessing and love:

> O my Love!
> on my bright and lovely *sari*
> there are so many loathsome stains
> its elegant face is ugly now
>
> xxx   xxx   xxx
>
> My Love brought me the soap of knowledge
> with it I wash the *sari* with care
> but the stains persist, leave it not.
> Says Kabir—I know the stains will go
> when my Love deigns to make me His own.   (L.S. 13)

Kabir has also expressed this sentiment in an inimitable way:

> Tortuous is the path of love
>
> xxx   xxx   xxx
>
> Says Kabir—if you drink from the cup of love
> you long to drink it more and more
> but it is far too hard to get
> the Dealer demands your head in lieu.
> If head you can yield
> treading on the path of love
> salvation you can have be sure.   (L.S. 16)

And in another song (not included here) Kabir has expressed the same view in a touching manner.

> Where do you seek Me O My man
> I am quite close to you!
> I am neither in temple nor in masjid

xxx   xxx   xxx

> Whoever wants me from core of heart
> with unalloyed love and earnest faith
> I am at once by his side.

This is comparable to what the Lord has declared in the Bhagvat Gita which is said to have been recounted by Him to Arjun the Pandav hero in the battle field in Mahabharat in the following words:

> I do not stay in the heavens
> nor in the heart of the anchorites
> O, Narada! I do stay where
> My devotees sing of Me!

This love has to be as intimate as that between the husband and the chaste wife, as true and deep as that. In the song at Sl. 39 Kabir has warned that:

> She alone can comprehend
> if her love for Him is true and deep
> but if not so
> futile will be all her make up.   (L.S. 39)

In yet another of his songs vide the reverse of the inner title page of the book Kabir declares that love is the Key to getting the Lord by superseding all erroneous thinking in the matter:

> The lock of error shuts the door
> of the mansion of your Love
> use the key of love and open
> the door and windows too
> and thus wake up your Love.
> Says Kabir—gentle folk listen
> you cannot get this chance again.

Like Kabir two other great Indian saint-poets who flourished in the wake of Kabir though not mystics like Kabir have also declared emphatically that it is not possible to get the Lord without deep and true love for Him.

Goswami Tulasi Das (16th century) of north India in his popular version of Ramayan the great Indian Epic, as Shri Rama Charit Manas says:

> milahi na raghupati binu anuraga—
> (Lord Rama is not attainable without Love)
> (Canto 7—Uttarkand)

and Mira (Rajasthan—contemporary of Tulasi) in one of her numerous love songs says—

> bina prem se na milae Nandalala—
> (without love none can aspire to get
> Nandalala, or Lord Krishna)

Kabir has by implication in most of his love songs in clear terms said that before the aspirant expects the Lord to pick him up and shower His love on him he must ensure that by offering his own love and devotion, and by surrendering to Him the aspirant has earnestly craved to win His love.

That strong being Kabir's conviction in the matter he has taken, as it will be easy to guess, all the pains to portray the tenets of true and deep love. For the master mind that Kabir was both as a poet and also as a spiritual thinker it was not at all incomprehensible or inexpressible.

And, when we remember his genuine concern for the well being and salvation of the mass of common man it is also easy to see that the portrayal had to be done not only in the diction of the common man but also in the ways of love he is familiar with.

And also when we come to think of love true and deep what is more expressive than the love between man and woman? And by all means that is what Kabir has portrayed in the songs, nothing more or nothing less.

The original songs in Devanagari script have been given on the left hand side page of the book and for the convenience of the reader unfamiliar with the Devanagari script, a transliteration in Roman script has been given under each of the originals.

In order to help the reader to read the transliteration in Roman script correctly a diacritical chart of pronunciation has been given in the introductory portion of the book.

G.N. Das

ACKNOWLEDGEMENTS

This humble work I have been able to do on Sant Kabir, I owe to the guidance and encouragement I received from the late Padmashree Dr. Ram Kumar Verma, Professor of Allahabad University fame, himself author of many books on the saint-poet.

But for the inspiration I got from Dr. Verma I would not have been able to translate over five hundred of Kabir's couplets (Dohas) and over a hundred of his love songs, all replete with spiritual message.

I am grateful to him for the message of appreciation for my humble work on Kabir.

I am beholden to the illustrious Dr. K.S. Duggal, former Chairman of the National Book Trust of India for having graciously agreed to write the foreword to this book of translation of one hundred love songs of Kabir.

I am thankful to Shri B.N. Pande, Member Rajya Sabha, and former Governor of Orissa State to have been a great source of encouragement and assistance to me in my efforts to write on Kabir and to have issued a message of good will for this book.

I am grateful to Shri B.R. Patel, a poet of national and international fame, to have not only agreed to write an illuminating Introduction, but also to have taken the pains to go through and brush up the poems where necessary.

G.N. Das

APPRECIATION

Excepts from appreciation by Padmashree Dr. Ram Kumar Verma of Allahabad University and widely known scholar and writer on Kabir

I am happy to record my appreciation to the translation of saint Kabir's poems made by Shri Gananath Das in the simple and expressive way in which Kabir himself wrote them.

Kabir through his message for the welfare of humanity has become an international poet and the translation made by Shri Das will be read and appreciated by readers in the west unfamiliar with Devanagari in which the poems are available.

I congratulate Shri Gananath Das for his remarkable work.

Lucknow   Dr. Ram Kumar Verma

MESSAGE

I am indeed happy that Shri Gananath Das of Bhubaneswar after writing a book on the biography and philosophy of Sant Kabir in Oriya prose, and translation into Oriya verse 100 of Kabir's poems and 100 of his Dohas, the book which I inaugurated in 1987 in Puri and being currently engaged in translation of Kabir's Dohas into rhymed English verse, has turned his attention to the love songs of Kabir one hundred of which he has translated into English in free verse style.

It is heartening to find Shri Das at his advanced age and retirement from a long spell of administrative service keeping up his zeal for dissemination of the message of the 15th century great saint-poet of Northern India, Sant Kabir.

The love songs of Kabir are a unique contribution of the saint-poet as a mystic poet of great renown. The central theme of the love songs is the urge of the soul *(Jivathma)* to unite with the Supreme Soul *(Paramathma)* or God. In this Kabir is said to have drawn upon the Hindu philosophical idea that soul is a part of the Supreme Soul and that it parted from the Supreme Soul under the *Lila* or Love-Game of God for ultimate reunion with the latter. It is for the soul to strive to achieve the reunion by means of ardent love for the Supreme Soul. Kabir has delineated this in his numerous captivating songs out of which Shri Das has selected and translated 100 in lucid free verse style.

According to Kabir man *(jiva)* has to help the process by creating and maintaining the proper condition and atmosphere for the soul to perform its part. By following the path of virtue, keeping the mind and heart clean he can render this help to the soul. On the other hand if he pursues a wrong track and sullies his character he hinders the process.

Kabir has again and again pointed out in his songs and Dohas, which are meant primarily for the benefit of his fellow-men, that devotion without love for the Lord is not devotion at all. He was so emphatic on this point that in one of his Dohas he said:

प्रेम बिना जो भक्ति है,
    सो निज दंभ विचार ।

"Prem binaa jo bhakthi hei
    So nija dambha bichaar"   [Kabir Doha]

And he has indicated too in his poems and Dohas that the two ways to attain salvation or union of soul with the Supreme Soul are (1) the way of the intellect or mind *(gyaan maarg)* and (2) through love or heart *(prem maarg)*. And Kabir has always given precedence to the way of love over the way of intellect. The following love song of Kabir and Shri Das's translation thereof confirms that:

भ्रम का ताला लगा महल रे, प्रेम की कुंजी लगावो ।
कपाट किवड़िया खोल के रे, यहि विधि पिया को जगावो ।
कहे कबीर सुनो भाइ साधो फिर न लागे अस दाव ॥

The lock of error shuts the door
of the mansion of your Love
use the key of love and open
the door and windows too
and thus wake up your Love.
Says Kabir–gentle folk listen
You cannot get this chance again.

In the words of Prof. Underhill the import of this song is that "the union (of soul with the Supreme Soul) is however brought about by love, not by knowledge or ceremonial observance".

It is obvious that in the love songs Kabir exhorts his fellowmen to strive for the ultimate objective of man which is to attain salvation for his soul or the union of soul and the Supreme Soul. This is apparent from not only the diction, imagery, and similes the common man is familiar with but also the way of love between man and woman he is conversant with, which Kabir has consistently used and referred to in his compositions.

The messages of Kabir are all contained in his songs and Dohas. In essence they emphasise two things in the main. First, to live a clean and contented life avoiding its pitfalls, and second, to strive for the union of Soul and the Supreme Soul through the way of love and self surrender to the Lord.

I congratulate Shri Das for having translated in a lucid and readable manner one hundred love songs of Kabir for the benefit of the English knowing readers.

I wish the efforts of Shri Das all success.

Raj Bhawan   B.N. Pande
Bhubaneshwar   Governor of Orissa
15 November, 1988

INTRODUCTION

They call him 'Kabir's man', a sobriquet anybody would be proud of. For Kabir is one of the most loved of the great saint-poets who have trodden the sacred soil of this ancient land, and Mr. G.N. Das has been writing for years about him and his teachings in the local newspapers in the local language and in a manner which the common people can understand. His publications include (1) Kabir—Life and Philosophy and (2) Kabir Shataka (One hundred hymns and one hundred couplets) both in Oriya. Besides, he has rendered into English verse over five hundred couplets, three hundreds of which are now under print. None would, therefore, deserve more than Mr. Das the encomium that the nickname so lovingly bestows upon him.

The present collection has one hundred poems which have been culled from the corpus commonly known as Kabir's love songs. In these poems Kabir sings of the Prem-lila of jivathma (the individual soul) and Paramathma (the Supreme Soul), of the ecstasy of love, wedlock and pangs of separation. Kabir conceives of *Jivathma* as a part of the *Paramathma* and sings of the longing of the part for union with the whole:

> Long long ago my soul parted
> from my Lord, the Soul Supreme
> and she craves union with Him
> but being unable is suffering
> severe pang of separation.   (Sl. 78)

We find the same urge in the following Doha:

> Says Kabir,
> The soul craves the Supreme Soul
>   To lose herself in Him
> Love-lorn the soul nears the goal
>   Quivering mingles in the Beam.
>   *(as translated by Mr. G.N. Das)*

In the Prem-lila of which he sings so ardently in these poems Kabir has assigned to the Jivathma the role of a woman, perhaps rightly so, because a woman's love is more urgent and more intense than a man's and a part has greater urge to unite with the whole like the drop of water vaporized falling into the ocean again at the first whiff of cold air.

And in India love follows the wedlock. Nothing has changed here since Kabir wrote the following lines—the maiden's song of welcome, the groom's procession, the vedic hymns, the sacred fire and the Saptapadi (the going round the fire seven times). And as if the world begins with marriage Das has chosen these lines to be the first poem of the collection:

> Young bride
> do sing the welcome song
> my Love has come to my hut today
>
> xxx   xxx   xxx
>
> My body I shall cause to be the altar
> where Brahma will chant the Vedas
> and with my Love
> I shall go round and round the sacred fire
> to celebrate my wedding with Him
>
> xxx   xxx   xxx
>
> Says Kabir: O my luck!
> I am going to wed my dear Love
> The Lord Supreme!   (Sl. 1)

And then the blissful conjugal life—the togetherness, the intimacy, the confidence and of course the game of dice! I remember the beautiful sculpture of Kailash, the rock-cut temple at Ellora—Shiva and Parvati are playing dice. Shiva is losing, he has lost several times and Parvati decides to call it a day and prepares to leave when Shiva with a bewitching smile and the index finger raised implores Parvati to play once more. Well, this is perhaps the picture of an ideal, happy conjugal life. But what would have happened had Parvati played the game wrongly or indifferently? Perhaps it would have been something like what Kabir has said:

> xxx   xxx   xxx
>
> If I cannot play the dice correctly
> at the crucial stage

> I shall fail to enter the home square
> to reach the Lord,
> And then I slide back
> to repeat the movement from square to square
> till I come back to the home square
> to either enter it or slide back again.
>
> (Sl. 71)

Kabir's love for his Lord is so intense that at times it borders on the sensual as in the following lines:

> O my Love! do come to my hut
> my body and mind are aching for You.
> When every one says I am Your spouse
> I feel ashamed and doubtful.
> So long as we have not joined our hearts
> and slept together in one bed
> how can I claim Your love my Dear?
>
> (Sl. 4)

Again

> my eyes are heavy with sleep my Love
> Come, let us go to bed.
>
> xxx   xxx   xxx
>
> Do step cautiously on to the bed, my Love
> my sister and aunt are still awake,
> Says Kabir—O gentle folk listen!
> for fear of others' ridicule
> I am shy of clinging to my Love!   (Sl. 43)

And how well expressed, how poetic is the jubilation:

> I shall light the lamp of love in me
> and sing the welcome song to Him
> I shall be with Him all night long
> basking in His bounteous love.   (Sl. 34)

How well matched are the words and the thought, flowing, spontaneous and unfettered, how apt the imagery!

Like many saint-poets of the Bhakti movement Kabir, too, believed that love is the only right path to lead to God:

> All the four lanes are fully blocked
> How can I go to meet my Love?
>
> xxx   xxx   xxx

33

> To surmount them
> I have been told to follow the paths
> of knowledge, devotion and penance.
> Says Kabir—O gentle folk listen!
> None can enter nor emerge
> Who does not know the way of Love (Sl. 91)

Again:

> The lock of error shuts the door
> of the mansion of your Lord.
> Use the key of love and open
> the door and windows too
> and gently wake up your Love. (Sl. 101)

And what is love?

> Love does not grow in field and forest
> nor is it sold in shop and market,
> But rich or poor you can have it
> if you sever your head
> and lay it at His feet.
> The saint, the fakir or the seer
> if he cannot his head surrender,
> from Love's doorstep he remains far.
>
> (Sl. 16)

Kabir's love for his God, then, is not what a father's love is for his children or a brother's for his sister. It is not even Krishna's love for Sudama or Sudama's for Krishna. It is different from companionship, friendship or camaraderie. Its only parallel can be found in the Gopis' love for Gopala. It's like a woman's love for her beloved, the deepest, the purest, the most soulful, love that asks for nothing in return, love that seeks no reciprocity; it only gives and gives until what turns out to be "pain for the other is pleasure for the lover". It is also the most rewarding in another sense, the reward being nothing less than "Mokshya", "Nirvana", the release from the cycle of deaths and births, union or merger with the Paramathma becoming Paramathma itself, Tat Tvam Asi. And there is nothing abstract in Kabir's love. It is the fountain-head of his humanism, his anguish for the suffering humanity as if he was the Tara of Tibetan Buddhism, born out of the tears of Avalokiteshwar, compassion-incarnate on earth:

> I weep on seeing
> The grind stone at work
> For, not a grain comes out whole
> From this grinding trap.

> Or
> Standing at the open market
> I crave for wellbeing of all.

It is like the cry of Bhima Bhoi, a nineteenth century tribal saint of Orissa:

> Out of my life's ashes
> Let mankind's deliverance dawn

or simply translated it would read:

> Let my life be consigned to Hell
> if that would redeem the world.

One of the finest examples of Kabir's universal brotherhood of man is found in the following oft quoted poem:

> If Khuda lives only in Masjid
> who looks after the rest of the world?
> If Raam is lodged in the temple idol
> who takes care of the universe?
> Is East the abode of Hari,
> and West that of Allah?
> Search in your heart for both of them,
> there live both Karim and Raam.
> They are one and the same,
> Creator of the universe
> men and women are His image
> and Kabir is son of both Raam and Karim,
> his preceptors are Guru and Pir alike.
>
> *(Translated by Das)*

How relevant is Kabir to the present day world torn by prejudices, intolerance and bigotry.

Rabindranath Tagore translated into English some of Kabir's poems including a few of his love songs in the year 1915. Some more have been translated since then. But as far as I know this is for the first time that a hundred of them have been put together in such translation. To translate Kabir into another Indian language may not be so very difficult as all the Indian languages share a common cultural heritage, beliefs and prejudices, have the same idiom and thought process. But to translate him into a foreign language like English is beset with many pitfalls. English has its own genius, its own idiom. The English sensibilities and the way they are expressed are not quite like ours. The difficulty is further compounded by the fifteenth century dialect in which Kabir sang.

While rendering poetry into another language, for the peculiarities involved, it is not so much translated as transcreated. Das, however, has not taken that much liberty with Kabir. His rendering is more close to literal translation than to transcreation.

Kabir is loved and read widely for his originality of thought and his spiritual and poetic excellence. He is quoted in learned discourses and in everyday conversation by the learned and not so learned alike. Kabir has entered into the subconscious of the Indian mind. He is a part of the common man's vocabulary. In this translation Das has tried to retain as much as possible the fluidity and spontaneity of expression, clarity and simplicity of the language and what is most important, the original flavour of Kabir and I have no doubt that it would help kindle among the English knowing readers both in the country and abroad an interest and curiosity to delve deeper into and know more about a unique, original and acutely sensitive mind.

Bhubaneshwar
4th August 1990

B.R. Patel

Diacriticals or guide to pronunciation (sound) of the Roman script transliteration of one hundred and one of the Love Songs of Kabir included in this book

a	=	अ				
aa	=	आ				
i	=	इ	dhha	=	ढ
ee	=	ई	nh	=	ण
u	=	उ	tha	=	त
uu	=	ऊ	thha	=	थ
e	=	ए	d	=	द
ei/ai	=	ऐ	dha	=	ध
o	=	ओ	na	=	न
owu	=	औ	pa	=	प
ka	=	क	pha	=	फ
kha	=	ख	ba	=	ब
ga	=	ग	bha	=	भ
gha	=	घ	ma	=	म
cha	=	च	ya	=	य
chha	=	छ	ra	=	र
ja	=	ज	la	=	ल
jha	=	झ	woh	=	व
ta	=	ट	sh	=	श
ttha	=	ठ	s	=	स
da	=	ड	ha	=	ह
			khya	=	क्ष

NO. 1

दुलहिनी गावहु मंगलचार ।
हम घरि आये परम पुरिस भरतार ।
तन रति करि मेैं मन रति करि हैं, पंच तत बराती ।
रामदेव मेरे पाहुन आये, मैं जोवन में माती ॥
सरीर सरोवर बेदी करि हैं, ब्रह्मा बेद उचारा ॥
रामदेव संग भँवरि लै हौं, धन धन भाग हमारा ॥
सूर तेतिस कोटिग आये, मुनियर सहस अठासी ॥
कहे कबीर हम ब्याहि चले हैं पुरिस एक अविनासी ॥

dulahani gaavahu mangalchaar
hum ghari aaye parum puris varthaar.
thun rathi kari mein mun rathi karihei punchthath baraathi,
raam dev mere paahun aaye main joban mein maathi.
sarir sarover vedi karihei brahmaa ved uchaaraa
raam dev sung vamvri leihon dhun dhun vaag humaaraa,
sura thethis kouthig aaye muniyer sahas athhaasi
kahe Kabir hum byaahi chalehein puris ek avinaasi.

Young bride
do sing the welcome song!
My Love has come to my hut today
in procession of the elements five.
He is my honoured guest tonight
my youth and love are welling up
I shall cling to Him in body and mind.
My body I shall cause to be the altar
where Brahma will chant the Vedas
and with my Love I shall go round and round
the sacred fire
to celebrate my wedding with Him
Gods and goddesses and countless sages
have come from far to see the wedding.
Says Kabir—O my luck!
I am going to wed my dear Love
The Lord Supreme!

NO. 2

वे दिन कब आवेंगे भाई ।
जा कारनि हम देह धरी हैं, मिलिबो अंग लगाई ।
हौं जानूं जे हिलमिल खेलूँ, तन मन प्राण समाई ।
या कामनां करो परिपूरण, समरथ हौं रामराई ।
माहिं उदासी माधौ चाहै, चितवन रैन बिहाई ।
सेज हमारी स्यंध भई है, जब सौं तब खाई ।
यहु अरदास दास की सुनिये, तन की तपन बुझाई ।
कहै कबीर मिलै जे सांई, मिल करि मंगल गाई ।

weh deen kub aawenge bhaai
jaa kaarani hum deha dhari hei milibo ung lagaayi.
hou jannu je hilmil khelun thun mun praan samaayi
Yah kaamanaa karou paripuran sumrath ho raam raayi.
maahi udaasi maadhou chaahei chith bun rein bihaayi.
sej humaari syndhh vayihei jub soun thub khaayi
yahu urdass daas ki suniye thun ki thapan bujhaayi
kahe Kabir miley je saayin mil kari mangal gaayi.

When will that day come round dear
for which I was born on earth
my Love, my Lord I shall embrace
clinging close and fast to Him
whisper words of tender love?
O my Almighty Lord Raam!
do fulfil this my eternal urge.
Waiting and waiting for You my Lord
I am passing the wakeful nights alone
my bedecked bed feels like a lion
that will devour me if I sleep thereon.
Do listen to Your slave's prayer
and relieve me of my agony.
Says Kabir—I shall doubtless get my Lord
and sing the auspicious song of love
in chorus with Him.

NO. 3

तलफै बिन बालम मोर जिया ।
दिन नहिं चैन रैन नहिं निंदिया ।
तलफ तलफ कै भोर किया ।
तन मन मोरा रहत अस डोलै ।
सुन्न सेज पर जनम छिया ।
नैन थकित पंथ न सुधै ।
सांइ बेदरदी सुध न लिया ।
कहत कबीर सुनो भाई साधो,
हर पीर दुख जोर किया ।

thulphe vin baalum mor jiyaa.
deen naahin chayen rein naahin nindiyaa
thulph thulph ke vor kiyaa.
thun mun mor rahath asa dolei
sunn sej per janum chhiyaa
nein thhakith bhaye panth na sudhe
saayin vedardi sudhi na liyaa
kahat Kabir suno vaai saadho
hara pir dukh jor kiyaa.

Intense is my agony
for want of my Love.
I am passing my days in great distress
and nights without a wink of sleep.
I lie all alone on my empty bed
waiting in suspense and bated breath
to hear my Love's footfall, but alas!
my eyes are dead tired of watching.
Says Kabir—I know not why
my Love is so unkind to me.
O gentle folk!
do some one help relieve my pain.

NO. 4

बालम आवौ हमरे गेह रे ।
तुम बिन दुखिया देह रे ॥
सब कोई कहत तुम्हारी नारी मो को इहै अंदेह रे ।
दिल से नाहिं दिल लगावो तब लग कैसा सनेह रे
एक मेक है सेज न सोये तब लग कैसा नेह रे ।
अन्न न भावै, नीन न आवै, घर बर धरै न धीर रे ।
कामिन है बालम प्यारा, ज्यों प्यासे को नीर रे ।
है कोइ ऐसा पर उपकारी, पिव से कहुं सुनाय रे ।
अब तो बेहाल कबीर भयो है, बिन देखे जीव जाय रे ॥

vaalum aawo humre geha re
thum bin dukhiyaa deha re.
sub koyi kahath thumhaari naari moko eehei undeha re
dil se naahi dil lagaayo thub lug keisaa sancha re
ek mek whe sej na soye thub lug keisaa neha re
anna na vaawe nin na aawe ghar var dhare na dhir re
kamin hei vaalum pyaaraa jyon pyaaseko neer re.
hey koi eysaa para upakaari peeb se kahu sunaay re
ub tho behaal Kabir vayo hei bin dekhe jeeb jaay re.

O my Love! do come to my hut,
my body and mind are aching for You.
When every one says I am Your spouse
I feel ashamed and doubtful;
So long we have not joined our hearts
and slept together in one bed
how can I claim Your love, my Dear?
I do not relish food, nor can I sleep
in my home I am always distraught.
As the thirsty longs for water
so is the love-lorn for her love.
Is there none to carry this message
to my Lord,
—Kabir is in great distress
pining and pining for his Love
he is going to die!

NO. 5

सुपने में सांई मिले सोवत लिया लगाय ।
आंख न खोलूँ डरपतां, मत सपना है जाय ।
सांई मेरे बहुत गुन, लिखे जो हिरदे मांहि ।
पिऊं न पानी डरपतां, मत वे धोये जाहिं ॥
नैना भीतर आव तूं, नैन झंपि तोहि लेउँ ।
ना मैं देखूं और कूं, ना तोहि देखन देउं ॥

supane mein saayin mileh sovat liyaa lagaay,
aankh na kholun durpataa muth sapnaa whey jaay.
saayin mere bohuth goon likhe jo hirde maahi,
piyun na paani darpataa muth weh dhoe jaahi,
naina vithar aawo thun nein jhaampi thohi leun,
naa mein dekhun worko naa, thohi dekhan deun.

In dream did my Lord come to me
I woke up to His tender touch.
To retain the bliss of my dream
I do not at all open my eyes.
My Lord inscribed His message of love
in the core of my little heart.
I do not at all drink any water
lest I should wash the message down.
Do come once inside my eye, my Love
I shall at once drop the lids
so I alone shall see You there
And none else You can see!

NO. 6

कौन मिलावै मोहि जोगिया हो ।
जोगिया बिन मोहि रह्या न जाय ।
हे हिरनी पिया पारधी हो मार सबद के बान ।
ताहि लागी सर जानहि हौ और दरद नहिं जान ।
मैं प्यासी हौं पिया की हौं रटत सदा पिब पीव ।
पिया मिलै तो जीव हौ ना तो सहजे त्यागौं जीव ।
पिय कारन पियरी भइ हौ लोग कहै तन रोग ।
छः छः लांघन मैं किया हो तन में मनहि मिलाय ।
तुम्हरी प्रीत के कारनै हौ बहुरि मिलैंगे आय ।

koun milaawe mohi jogiya ho
jogiyaa vin mohi rahyaa na jaay.
hei hirni piyaa pardhi ho maar sabad ke baan
thaahi laagi sur jaan hi ho wor dard naahin jaan,
mein pyaasi houn piyaaki ho ratath sadaa piv piv
piyaa mile thoh jiv hou naa thoh sahje thyaagon jiv.
piyaa kaarun piyaari vai hou log kahe thun rog
chhaha chhaha langhan mein Kiyaa hou
thun mein mun hi milaay
tumahrey prith ke kaarn hou bohuri milenge aaye.

Who can help me meet my Love?
My mind is always aching for Him.
How can I survive?
Expert archer is my Love
With His unfailing arrows of words.
They have touched and pierced my heart
and now my ache is gone.
I am pining for Him always
chanting always "O Love, O my Love."
I shall survive if I get Him
or else I shall succumb.
I am love-sick for my Lord
But people say I am sick of body!
Only to get Him I am distraught
forgetful of all decorum.
Says Kabir—O sister listen!
Enamoured of your abiding love
The Lord will seek you out be sure.

44

NO. 7

मैं का से बुझौं अपने पिया की बात सैं ।
जान सुजान प्रानप्रिय प्रिय बिन, सबै बटाऊ जात री ।
आसा नदी अगाध कुमति बहै, रोकि काहु पें न जात री ।
काम क्रोध दोउ भये करारे, पड़ें बिसय रस मात री ।
जे पांचे अपमान के संगी, सुमिरन को अलसात री ।
कहे कबीर बिछुरि नहिं मिलिहे, ज्यों तरवर बिन पात री ।

mein kaa sei bujhoun apne piya ki baathari
jaan sujaan praan priya priyaa vin sabei baataaun jaathari
aasaa nadi agaadh kumati bahe roki kahupei na jaathari
kaam krodh dou vaiye karaare padey bisay rus maathari
ja paanche apamaan kei sungi, sumiran kou alsaathari
kahe Kabir bichhudi naahi milihey jyon tharabar vin paatari.

Who shall I enquire
about my Love?
Dearer than life is He to me
without Him I shall forsake all
and become a street beggar.
Reckless runs the crooked stream of longings
none can curb its flow.
Lust and ire, two enemies dire
plunge one in the sea of vice
and when all the five and jealousy join
you lose all your zeal for Him
Says Kabir—O gentle folk do ponder
can leaf once detached rejoin the tree?

NO. 8

बहुत दिनन ते मैं प्रीतम पाये
भाग बड़े घर बैठे आये ।
मंगल चार माहिं मन राखौं
राम रसायन रसवा चाखों ।
मंदिर माहिं भया उजियारा
ले सती अपना पीव पियारा ।
मैं रानी रासी कै निधि पाई
हमहि कहावहु तुमहि बड़ाई ।
कहै कबीर मैं कछु न कीन्हा
सखी सुहाग राम मोहि दीन्हा ।

bohuth dinan thei mein pritum paaye
bhaag badi ghur baithe aaye.
mangal chaar maahin mun raakhoun
raam rasaayan rasanaa chaakhoun
mandir maahi vaiyi ujiyaaraa
leh sati apanaa pib piyaaraa
mein rani raasi kei nindhi paayi
humhi kahaayahu thumahi badaayi
kahe Kabir mein kachhu na kinhaa
sakhi suhaag raam mohi dinhaa.

After a long wait have I got my Love
What luck! He himself did come home.
I shall sing the welcome song
steeped in the Nectar of His Name.
My Lord, my Love, He has come!
My heart is shining in His glow
I shall place Him on the throne there.
My precious Love I have got today!
without my effort it is all His grace
my Love, my Raam put the consort's mark
on my face.

NO. 9

चल हंसा वा देस जँह पिया बसैं चितकोर ।
सुरत सोहागिन हैं पनिहारिन भरै ठाड़ बिन डोर ॥
वाहि देसवा बादल ना उमड़ै रिमझिम बरसै मेह ।
चौबारे में बैठ रहना जा भीजेहुँ निर्देह ॥
वाहि देस में नित पूर्णिमा कबुहं न होय अंधेर ।
एक सुरज के कवन बतावे, कोटिन सूरज उजेंर ॥

chal hansaa waah desh jahan piyaa basei chithkor
surath sohagin hei panihaarin varei thhaad vin dor.
waahi deshwaah baadal na umadei rim jhim varase meha
chouwaare mein baithhe rahanaa jaa bhijehu nirdeha
waahi desh mein nith poornima kabahu na hoi andher
ek suraj ke kaban bathaawe kotin surj ujer.

O Swan! let us fly to that land
where my Love is the Monarch,
Without rope and bucket the maids
draw water there from the well.
Without cloud it rains there
that will drench our bodiless form,
Full moon shines there every night
Every day is sunny and bright
With myriad suns' effulgence.

NO. 10

अरे दिल

प्रेम नगर का अंत न पाया, ज्यों आया त्यों जावेगा ।
सुन मेरे साजन सुन मेरे मीता, या जीवन में क्या क्या बीता ।
सिर पाहन का बोझा लीता, आगे कौन छुड़ावेगा ।
परली पार मेरा मीत खड़िया, उस मिलन का ध्यान न धरिया ।
टूटी नाव ऊपर जो बैठा, गाफिल गोता खावैगा ।
दास कबीरा कहै समुझाई, अंत नाल तेरा कौन सहाई ।
चला अकेला संग न कोई, किया अपना पावैगा ।

aare dil prem nagarkaa antha na paaya
jyyun aayaa thyun jawegaa.
suun mere saajan suun mere mitha
yaa jiban mein kyaa kyaa bithaa
shir paahan kaa bojhaa lithaa
aage koun chhudawegaa.
parlipaar meraa meeth khadiyaa
ush milan kaa dhhyyaan na dhariya
tuti naab upar jo baithaa
gaafil gotha khaawegaa.
daas Kabiraa kahe samajhaayi
anta naal theraa koun sahaayi
chalaa akelaa sung na koyi
kiyaa apanaa pawegaa.

O my mind!
You do not yet know the city of your Love
Just as you have come from there
So you shall go back!
Tell me, my friend
What all you did in life
Why are you carrying a heavy load,
who will relieve you of it?
Look my Love is waiting on the other shore
you pay no heed to that meeting!
You are on a fragile boat
unmindful of what may befall.
And for your foolishness
you will deserve kicks.
Who will aid you in the end?
Beware! you shall go back all alone
Carrying the outcome of all your deeds.

NO. 11

कैसे दिन कटिहै जतन बताइ जइयो ।
यहि पार गंगा वहि पार जमुना
बिचवा हमके मढ़इया छवाये जइयो ।
अचिरा खारि के कागद बनाइन
अपनि सुरतिया हियरे लगाये जइयो ।
कहत कबीर सुनो भाई साधो
बहिया पकरिके राहिया बताइये जइयो ।

keise deen katihei jathan bataayi jayiyo.
yahi paar gangaa wahi paar yamunaa
bichwaa humke madhaiyaa chhabaaye jaiyiyo.
achiraa khaari ke kaagad banaayin
apani suratiyaa hiyare lagaaye jayiyo.
kahat Kabir suno bhaai saadho
bahiyaa pakarike raahiya bathayiea jayiyo.

O my Love, come tell me how
I shall spend my days on earth.
Between the Ganges and Yamuna
is my little hut
do come and get its roof rethatched.
I have torn a piece of my *saari*
do draw on it the comely picture
of your winsome face
and paste it on my bare chest.
Says Kabir—do take hold of my arm, my Love
and show me the right path to You.

NO. 12

मोहि तोहि लागी कैसे छूटे ।
जैसे कमल पत्र जल वासी
ऐसे तुम साहब हम दासी ।
जैसे चकोर तकत निसि चंदा
ऐसे तुम साहब हम बंदा ।
मोहि तोहि आदि अंत बन आई
अब कैसे लगन दुराई !
कहे कबीर हमर मन लाई
जैसे सरिता सिंध समाई ।

mohi thohi laagi keise chhute.
jeise kamal pathra jal baasaa
yiese thum saahaab hum daasaa
jeise chakor thakath nisi chandaa
yiese thum sahaab hum bundaa
mohi thohi aadi anth bani aayee
ub keise lagan duraayee?
kahe Kabir humar mun laayi
jeise sarithaa sindh samaayi.

How can our link snap, my Love?
As the lotus leaf clings to water
so I am Your slave, You are my Master.
Like the night-bird's vigil on the moon
my eyes are glued to Your feet.
You are my Lord since eternity
can such a bond ever snap?
Says Kabir—my mind is filled with joy,
I shall mingle in His beam
as does the stream in the sea!

NO. 13

मेरी चुनरी में परिगयो दाग पिया ।
पांच तत की बनी चुनरिया
सोरह सौ बैद लाग किया ।
यह चुनरी मेरे मैके ते आयी
ससुरे में मनवा खोय दिया ।
मल मल धोये दाग न छूटे
ग्यान का साबुन लाये पिया ।
कहत कबीर दाग तब छुटि है
जब साहब अपनाय लिया ।

meri chunri mein parigayo daag piyaa.
panchthatha ki bani chunariyaa
sorah so vaid laage kiyaa
yaha chunri mere maikethe aayi
sasure mein munwaa khoy diyaa.
mul mul dhoeye daag na chhute
gyaan kaa sabun laaye piyaa
kahath Kabir daag thub chutihei
jub sahab apanaaye liyaa.

O my Love!
On my bright and lovely *saari*
there are so many loathsome stains
its elegant face is ugly now.
A band of sixteen hundred experts
made this *saari* with the elements five.
I got this from my father's house
in my in-law's house here
I failed to take its care.
My love brought me the soap of knowledge
with it I wash the *saari* with care
but the stains persist, leave it not.
Says Kabir—I know the stains will go
when my Lord deigns to make me His own.

NO. 14

जियरा मेरे फिरे रे उदास ।
राम बिन निकस जाई सांस आजहुँ कौन आस ।
जहाँ जहाँ जाउं राम मिलावे ना कोई
कहो संतो कैसे जीवन होई ।
जरै सरीर तपन कोइ न बुझावै
अनल दहे निस नींद न आवै ।
चंदन घस घस अंग लगाऊं
राम बिन दारून दुख पाऊं ।
सत संगति मति करि धीरा
सहज जानि रामहि भजै कबीरा ।

jiyaraa mere phire re udaas
raam bin nikas jayi saans aajahu koun aash.
jahaan jahaan jaaun raam milaawe na koyi
kaho santho keise jiban hoyee,
jare sharir thapan koyi na bujhaawe,
anul dahe nisa neend na aawe
chandan ghus ghus anga lagaaun
raam bin daarun dukh paayun
suth sangathi mathi mun kari dhiraa
sahaj jaani raamahi vajey Kabiraa.

I seek Him here and there all over
but in vain
I do not find my Raam anywhere.
How without Him
can I live any more?
Who can say for not getting Him
my breath will not stop today?
No one helps me meet my Raam,
O gentle soul!
say how can I keep alive?
My body burns like on fire
it keeps me awake the whole of night
the sandal paste does hardly abate
its burning sensation.
All day I roam all night awake
how can I endure?
Says Kabir—O my mind
stay staid and alert
in your devotion to the Lord
your enternal Love!

NO. 15

प्रेम का मारग बांका रे ।
वह जानत है सीस प्रेम में अर्पण जाकारे ।
यह तो घर है प्रेम का, खाला का घर नाहिं
सीस काट चरनन धरौ, तब पैठे घर माहिं ।
देखी कायर मन संकारे, प्रेम का मारग बांका रे ।
प्रेम पियाला जो पिये, सीस दखिना देय
लोभी सीस न दे सकें, नाम प्रेम का लेय ।
प्रेम न बाड़ी ऊपजै, प्रेम न हाट बिकाय
राजा परजा जो चहै, सिर सांटे ले जाय ।
जोगी जंगम सेबड़ा, सन्यासी दरवेश
प्रेम बिना पहुंचे नहीं, दुरलभ सतगुरु देस ।
प्रेम पियाला नाम का, चाखत अधिक रसाल
कबीर पीना कठिन है, मांगै सीस कलाल ।
मिले तेहि मुक्ति का नाकारे, प्रेम का मारग बांका रे ।

prem kaa maarug baankaa re
woh jaanath hei shis prem mein arpan jaakaa re.
yah tho ghar hei prem kaa khaalaa kaa ghar naahin
shis kaat charunun dharei thub paithhe ghur maahin
dekhi kaayar mun sankaa re, prem kaa maarug baankaa re,
prem piyaalaa jo piyaa shis dakshinaa dey
lovi shis na de sake naam prem ki ley.
prem naa baadi upaje, pre naa haati bikaay
rajaa parajaa jo chaahei shir sante leh jaay.
jogi jangum sebadaa sanyasi durvesh
prem binaa pahunche naahi durlav sathgur desh.
prem piyalaa naam kaa chaakhth adhik rasaal
Kabir pinaa kathhin hei maage shis kalaal
mile thehi mukti ka nakaa re, prem kaa maarug bankaa re.

Tortuous is the path of love
he alone who surrenders his head
has the right to tread
and he knows what it is.
This is abode of love my dear
and not the aunt's dwelling house
that you can enter at your will.
You have the access only if
you sever and lay your head at His feet
the timid shivers to think of it.
You can drink from the cup of love
only if you can offer your head
that is the only way to win
the path of love is uneven.
The miser cannot offer his head
he can only talk of it.
Love does not grow in field and forest
nor is it sold in shop and market.
But rich or poor you can have it
if you sever your head
and lay it at His feet.
The saint, the Fakir or the seer
if he cannot his head surrender
from Love's doorstep he remains far.
Says Kabir—if you drink from the cup of Love,
you long to drink it more and more
but it is far too hard to get
the Dealer demands your head in lieu.
If head you can yield
treading on the path of love
salvation you shall have for sure.

NO. 16

रैन गई मति दिन भी जाई ।
भँवर उड़ै बग बैठे आई ।
कांचे कड़वे रहे न पानी
हंस उड़्या काया कुमलानी ।
थर थर थर थर कांपै जीव
ना जांनू का करिहै पीव ।
कौवा उड़ावत मेरि बहियां पिरानी
कहै कबीर मेरो कथा सिरानी ।

raiyen gayi mathi deen vih jaayi
vambar uddey baga baithhe aayi
kanche kadwe rahe naa paani
huns udayaa kaayaa kumlaani
thur thur thur thur kaampe jiv
naa jaanu kaa karihei peeb
kaawaa udaawath meri bahiyaan piraani
kahe Kabir mero kathaa siraani.

Night has ended
Let not day too end in vain.
The beetle is bidding the flowers adieu
the crane has come and is sitting still.
As a pot of unbaked clay
cannot hold water,
a lifeless body is useless.
I know not what my Love will do
so I am quaking in constant fear.
My arms are tired of scaring the crow
to know what is in my Love's mind
and what is going to befall me.

NO. 17

हम सौ रहया न जाय मुरलिया की धुन सुनि कै ।
बिन बंसत फुल एक फूलै, भँवर सदा बुलाय ।
गगन गरजे बिजरी चमकै उठत हिये हिलोर ।
बिगसत कँवल मेघ बरसाने चितवत प्रभु की ओर ।
तारी लागी तहां मन पहुँचा गैब धुजा फहराय ।
कहै कबीर आज प्रान हमारा जीवत ही मरजाय ।

hum soun rahyaa na jaay muraliyaa ke dhun suni ke.
bin basant phul eek phuley vambar sadaa bulaay
gagan garaje bijli chamakeh uthhath hiye hillor
bigasath kamal megh barasaane chithbuth pravuki orr
thari laagi thahaan mun pohunchaa gaib dhujaa phaharaay
kahe Kabir aaj praan humaaraa jibath hee mur jaay.

I cannot remain an instant here
I must arise and go there now
where sweet music swells from His flute
and lotus blooms all the year round,
and bees raise a constant hum.
Clouds gather there in the sky
with streaks of lightning threading them
and rains pour down
on the blooming lotus.
A unique wave wells up in me
I shiver and yearn for the Lord.
Remaining staid my mind reaches
where the Lord's flag flutters on His shrine!
O Lord! let me at this moment die!!

NO. 18

तोहि मोहि लगन लगाय रे फकीरवा ।
सोवत ही मैं अपने मंदिर में
सबद बान मारि जगाये रे फकीरवा ।
डूबत ही भव के सागर में
बहियां पकरि समुझाये रे फकीरवा ।
एकै बचन बचन नहिं दूजा
तुम मोसे बंद छुड़ाये रे फकीरवा ।
कहे कबीर सुनो भाई साधो
प्राणन प्राण लगाये रे फकीरवा ।

thohi mohi lagan lagaaye re Fakirwaa
sobath hi mein apne mandir mein
sabda baan maari jagaaye re Fakirwaa.
dubath hi bhaba ke saagar mein
bahiyaan pakari samujhaaye re Fakirwaa.
ekei bachan bachan naahin dujaa
thum moshe bundh chhudaayere Fakirwaa.
kahe Kabir suno bhaai saadho
praanun praan lagaayere Fakirwaa.

You linked us together O, Fakir,
I was deep asleep in my cottage,
Your words of love
struck my ear and woke me up.
I was drowning in the sea of vice,
You pulled me out by my arm.
Your counsel sank into my heart
and in moments freed me
from earthly bonds.
Says Kabir—O gentle soul listen,
The Fakir embraced me in a hug
and pressed my heart close to His.

NO. 19

रितु फागुन नियरानी,
कोई पिय से मिलावै
पिया को रूप कहां लग बरनूं
रूपहि माहिं समानी ।
जो रंग रंगे सकल छवि छाके
तन मन सभी भुलानी ।
जो मत जानै याहिरे फाग है
यह कछु अकथ कहानी ।
कहै कबीर सुनो भाइ साधो
यह गत बिरलै जानी ।

ritu phagun niyaraani,
koyi piyaa se milaawe
piyaa ko roop kahaan lug baranu
rupahi maahi samaani
jo rung rungey sakal chaabi chaake
thun mun savi bhulaani
jo muth jaanei yahire phaag hei
yaha kachu akathh kahaani
kahe Kabir suno bhaai sadho
yaha guth birle jaani.

The spring season is come my dear
Do help me meet my Love!
Who can narrate His grace and charm?
He is source of all beauty.
The most gifted artist
has wrought His frame!
It wins the mind and heart in trice.
And Lo! His grace, beauty, and charm
is itself spring!
And that is incomprehensible.
Says Kabir—O gentle soul listen,
few comprehend this.

NO. 20

कौन मुरली सबद सुनि आनंद भयो ।
जोत बरै बिन बाती ।
बिना मूल के कमल प्रगट भये
फुलवा फूलत भांति भांति ।
जैसे चंद्रमा चकोर चितवै
जैसे चातक स्वाती ।
तैसे संत सूरत के हो के
हो गये जनम संगाती ।

koun murali subda suni aanand bhayo
joth barei bin baathi
bin mul ke kamal pragat bhayo
phulwaa phulath vaathi vaathi
jeise chandramaa chakor chitawe
jeise chathak swathi
theise sant surath ke ho ke
ho gaye janum sungaathi.

Whose flute is it
that fills my heart with joy?
The flame is burning without a wick,
the lotus is blooming without a root
flowers of many a hue are blooming.
As the night-bird gazes at the moon
as the rain-bird waits for the *swaati* rain,
so has the beloved fixed her mind
on her Love's feet eternally.

NO. 21

नारद प्यार सौं अंतर नाहीं ।
प्यार जागै तो हिं जागूं प्यार सोवै तब सोऊं
जो कोइ मोर प्यार दुखावै जड़ मूल सों खोऊं ।
जहां मेरे प्यार जस गावै तहां करौं मैं बासा
प्यार चलै आगे उठ धाऊं मोहि प्यार की आसा ।
बेहद तीरथ प्यार के चरननि कोटि भक्त समाय
कहै कबीर प्रेम की महिमा प्यार देत बुझाय ।

Narad pyaar soun anther naahin
pyaar jaage tho hin jaagun payaar sobe thub soun
jo koi mere pyaar dukhaawe jud mul so khoun.
jahaan mere pyaar jush gaawe thahaan karoun mein baasaa
pyaar chale aage uthh dhaaun mohi pyaar ki ashaa.
behud thirath pyaar ki charanani koti vaktha sammay.
kahe Kabir prem ki mahima pyaar deth bujhaay.

I shall not leave my Love alone.
When He gets up shall I awake
and sleep only when He goes to bed.
Whoever pains my Love I shall
be rigid and speak not a word to him.
Wherever my Love's praise is sung
there shall I build me a hut
and if He leaves the place I shall
run ahead to be near Him,
never to lose from sight.
In the August feet of my Love
do all the sacred places rest
and countless devotees take shelter.
Says Kabir—my Love explained to me
the import of His Love!

NO. 22

आज दिन के मैं जाऊं बलिहारी ।
पीतम साहब आये मेरो पाहुना
घर आंगन लागै सुहौवना ।
सब प्यास लागे मंगल गायन,
भये मगन लखि छवि मन भावन ।
चरन पखारूं बदन निहारूं
तन मन धन सब साईं पै वारूं ।
या दिन पाये पिया धन सोइ
होत आनंद परम सुख होइ ।
सुरत लागि सतनाम की आसा
कहै कबीर दासन के दासा ।

aaj deen ke mein jaaun balihaari
pitam saahub aaye mero paahunaa
ghur aangan laage suhounaa.
sub pyaas laage mangal gaayan
vaye magan lakhi chhavi mun vaawan.
charan pakhaarun badan nihaarun
thun mun dhun sub sayin pe baarun.
vaa deen paaye piya dhun soyi
hoth aanand param sukh hoyi
surath laagi suth nam ki aashaa
kahe Kabir daasan ke daasaa.

I am steeped in the sea of joy today
My Love is the honoured guest to me
the entire house shines in His glow
my heart throbs and dances in great glee
seeing His uncommon winsome face.
I sing the melodious welcome song
wash His feet and look into His eyes
and offer my body and heart to Him.
Today I have got my precious Love
my mind and heart dance in joy.
Says Kabir—with devout love I meditate Him
and repeat His name as His slave.

NO. 23

समझ देख मन मीत पियरवा
आशिक हो कर सोना क्या रे ?
पाया हो तो दें ले प्यारे
पाय पाय फिर खोना क्या रे ?
रूखा सूखा गम का टुकड़ा
फीका और सलोना क्या रे ?
जब अंखियन में नींद घनेरी
तकिया और बिछौना क्या रे ?
कहे कबीर प्रेम का मारग
सिर देना तो रोना क्या रे ?

samujh dekh mun mith piyarwaa
aashik ho kur sonaa kyaa re.
payaa hei thoh de le pyaare
paay paay phir khona kyaa re.
rukhaa sukhaa gumkaa tukdaa
phikaa wor salonaa kyaa re.
jub aankhiyun mein neend ghaneri
thakiyaa wor bichhona kyaa re.
kahe Kabir prem kaa maarug
shir denaa thoh ronaa kyaa re.

O my mind, my friend, do ponder!
Is it worthwhile for the beloved
to beguile herself in heedless slumber?
If you have given yours
and got His love,
can you afford to lose it, dear?
If dry bread pieces are all your fare
will salty or saltless taste really matter?
If you are benumbed by slumber
can you wait for cushion or cover?
Says Kabir—unique is the path of love
if you can sever your head
why need you shed a tear?

NO. 24

परबति परबति मैं फिरया नैन गँवाये रोइ
सो बूटी पाऊं नहीं जाते जीवन होइ ।
नैन हमारे जलि गये छिन छिन लोड़ू तुझ
ना तुम मिलो ना मैं सुखी ऐसी बेदन मुझ ।
सुखिया सब संसार है, खाये और सोये
दुखिया दास कबीर है जागे अरू रोवे ।

parbathi parbathi mein phiryaa nein gambaaye royi
so buti paaun naahin jaathe jibun hoyi.
nayen humaare jali gaye chhin chhin lodu thujh
naa thum mileh naa mein sukhi eise bedun mujh.
sukhiyaa sub sansaar hei khaaye wor sowe
dukhiyaa daas Kabir hei jaage wor rowe.

I have roamed the mountains, hills and dales
searched all the nook and corner
I have not got the panacea
that can make my life secure.
Tears have blinded my tired eyes,
they are burning as though on fire.
I am searching always for my Love
I do not get Him, it pains me so.
All the world is in happiness
eating and sleeping soundly,
Kabir alone is steeped in grief
weeping and sleepless all night through.

NO. 25

कछु लेना न देना मगन रहना ।
पांच तत्त का बना पींजरा
जा में बोले है तेरो मैना ।
गहरी नदिया नाव पुरानी
केवटिया से मिले रहना ।
तेरो पिया तेरे घट में बसत है
सखी खोल कर देखो नैना ।
कहै कबीर सुनो भाइ साधो
गुरू के चरनन लिपट रहना ।

kacchu lenna na denaa magun rahanaa.
paanch thath kaa banaa pinjraa
jaamein bolehei thero maynaa
gahari nadiyaan naab puraani
kebatiyaa se mile rahnaa.
there piyaa there ghut mein basath hei
sakhi khol kur dekho nainaa.
kahe Kabir suno bhaayi saadho
guru ke charanan lipat rahanaa.

No give and take of the world, my mind
be immersed in the love of the Lord.
Your body is the cage, listen!
built of the elements five,
inside it is your parrot singing.
Deep and reckless runs the river of life
and fragile is your boat,
take shelter of the Oarsman, dear.
Your Love, the Lord is within you
open your eyes to see Him there.
Says Kabir—O gentle folk listen!
do catch hold of the Guru's feet.

NO. 26

तुम बिन राम कवन सों कहिये
लागी चोट बहुत दुख सहिये ।
बेध्यो जीव बिरह के भालै
रात दिवस मेरो उर सालै ।
को जानै मेरे तन की पीरा
सतगुरू सबद बहि गयो सरीरा ।
तुम सूं बैद ना हमसूं रोगी
उपजै व्यथा कैसे जीवै वियोगी ।
निसि बासर मोहि चितवत जायी
अजहुँ न आइ मिलै राम राई ।
कहत कबीर हमको दुख भारी
दरसन बिन क्यूं जीवहि मुरारी ।

thum bin raam kaban soun kahiye
laagi chot bohuth dukh sahiye
bedhyo jeeb birah ki vaalei
raat dibas mero ur saalei.
ko jaane meraa thun ki piraa
sath guru savud vahi gayo sarira.
thumh soun bayed na hamasoun rogi
upaje byathaa keise jibei viyogi
nisi baasuri mohi chithbuth jaayi
ajahu na aayi meiley raamarayi.
kahath Kabir humko dukh bhaari
darshan bin qun jibahi muraari.

Lord Raam, my Love!
who save You shall I tell my sorrow?
The pain I am suffering for want of You,
the pang of separation is too acute
its constant ache is killing me.
I survive by Your Name alone
the kind Guru gave it as a boon to me.
For relief of my torment, my Love
Your healing touch is the only cure.
Day and night I remain distraught
for not getting my Love, my Raam.
Says Kabir—my pain is so acute
without You, my Love, how can I endure?

NO. 27

तो को पिया मिलेंगे घूंघट के पट खोल रे ।
घट घट में वोहि साईं रमते
कटुक बचन मत बोल रे ।
धन जौबन का गरब न कीजै
झूठा पंचरंग चोल रे ।
सुन्न महल में दिया बार लै
आसा सौ मत डोल रे ।
जोग जुगत सों रंगमहल मे
पिया पाये अनमोल रे ।
कहै कबीर आनंद भयो है
बाजत अनहद ढोल रे ।

tho ko piyaa milenge ghunghat ke pat khol re.
ghut ghut mein wohi saayin ramathey
katuk vachan muth bol re
dhun jobun kaa garab na kijey
jhu-thhaa punch rung chol re
sunna mahal mein diyanaa baar le
aashaa soun muth dol re
jog jugath so rung mahal mein
piyaa paayeh unmol re.
kahe Kabir aanand vayo hei
baajath anahud dhol re.

Remove the veil
you will meet your gracious Lord.
In every being does He reside
never be harsh to any, my dear.
Do not be proud of your wealth and youth,
human life is transient.
In the void of your heart
light the lamp and wait for Him
with hope and confidence.
Your precious Lord will come there
and you will get Him all for you.
Says Kabir—be happy and alert, dear
lend your ear to the music swelling
from the celestial drum!

NO. 28

अजहुँ बीच कैसे दरसन तेरा
बिन दरसन मन माने क्यूं मोरा ।
हमहिं कुसेवक क्या तुमहिं अजाना
दुहि में दोस कहौ किन रामा ।
तुम कहियत त्रिभुवन पति राजा
मन बांछित सब पुरवत काजा ।
कहै कबीर हरि दरस दिखावै
हमहिं बुलावै कौ तुम्ह चलि आवे ।

aajhun beech keise darsun theraa
bin darsun mun maane qun moraa?
humhi kusebuk kya thumahi ajaanaa
duhi mein dosh kaho kina raamaa?
thum kahiyath thrivuvan pathi raajaa
mun banchhith sub purabath kaajaa
kahe Kabir hari darus dikhaawe
humhin bulaawe kou thumha chali aawe.

I must somehow see You today.
I cannot be happy without You.
If I am not Your faithful slave
do You or do not know that much?
Both of us cannot be in error?
Raam, my Love, is the Monarch
of all the universe,
He can fulfil all desires.
Says Kabir—my Lord do show Your face
whenever I call respond at once.

NO. 29

परोसनि मांगै कंत हमारा
पिव क्यूं बौरि मिलहि उधारा ।
मासा मांगै रती न देऊं
घटै मोरा प्रेम तो कासनि लेऊं ।
राखि परोसनि लरिका मोरा
जो कछु पाऊं सो आधा तोरां ।
बन बन ढूंढे नैन भरि जोऊं
पीव न मिलै तो बिलखि करि रोऊं ।
कहै कबीर यह सहज हमारा
बिरला सुहागिन कंत पियारा ।

parosani maage kunth humaaraa
pib qun bouri milahi udhaaraa!
maasaa maage rati na deun
ghate moraa prem thoh kaasein leun?
raakhi parosani larikaa moraa
jo kuchhu paaun so aadhaa thoraa.
bun bun dhunde nayun vari joun
pib na mile tho bilakhi kari roun.
kahe Kabir yaha sahaj humaaraa
birlaa suhaagin kunth piyaaraa.

My neighbour begs to borrow my Love
she is mad and unknowing,
does any one ever lend her Love?
Even if she begs a hundred times
I will not spare my Love at all.
She should know if my love wanes
who shall I beg to make it up?
Or else how can I gain my Love?
If she takes care of my worries
some of my gains I may concede,
But never can I lend my Love.
I am myself in search of Him
in hills and dales and forests deep
I am weeping my eyes out in sorrow
Says Kabir—I believe at heart my dear
scarce is the beloved who gains His favour.

NO. 30

अब तोहि जान न देहुं राम पियारे ।
ज्यूं भावै त्यूं होइ हमारे ।
बहुत दिनन के बिछुरे हरि पाये
भाग बड़े घर बैठे आये ।
चरननि लागौं करौं बरिआई
प्रेम प्रीत राखौं उरझाई ।
इत मन मंदिर रहौ नित चौसे
कहे कबीर परहु मति घौसे ।

ub thohi jaan na deun raam piyaare
jyun bhaawe thun hoyi humaare.
bohuth dinan ke bichhure hari paaye
bhaag bade ghur baithe aaye.
charanani laagoun karoun bariaayi
prem prith rakhoun urajhaayi.
itha mun mundir raho nith chouse
kahe Kabir parahu mathi ghouse.

I will not let You go my Raam, my Love,
do stay with me as it would behove.
I am getting You after too long a wait
in my little cottage, what luck!
I shall wash Your feet and welcome You
install You in my heart's chamber
and keep You bound by the bond of Love.
Says Kabir—O my Lord, my Love
do stay in the temple of my heart
in the way You would like best!

NO. 31

कब देखौं मेरे राम सनेही ।
जा बिन दुख पावै मोरी देही ।
हौं तेरा पथ निहारूं स्वामी
कब मिलेहिंगे मेरे अंतरजामी ।
जैसे जल बिन मीन तलफै
ऐसे हरि बिन मेरा जियरा कलपै ।
निस दिन हरि बिन नींद न आवै
दरस पिआसी राम क्यूं सचु पावै ।
कहै कबीर अब बिलम न कीजै
अपनी जानि मोहि दरसन दीजै ।

kub dekhun mere raam sanehi
jaa bin dukh paawe mori dehi
hou theraa puth nihaarun swaami
kub milehige anteryaami.
jeise jal bin min thalafei
eise hari bin mere jiyaraa kalapey.
nis din hari bin nid na aawe
darus piyaasi raam qun sachu paawe
kahe Kabir ub bilum na kije
apani jaani mohi darasun deeje.

When shall I see You my Raam, my Love?
Untold grief I suffer for want of You!
O my Lord, You know it all,
for ages I am waiting for You
when will You deign to come to me?
Sleepless days and nights I am passing
like fish out of water my heart is aching
steeped I am in sorrow without You
how soon shall I see You, O, my Love?
Says Kabir—my Lord, now do not tarry
I am Your own, do come, do hurry!

NO. 32

आयो दिन गौने कै हो मन होत हुलास ।
डोलिया उठावै बिजा बनवा हो
जहां कोइ ना हमार ।
पयां तेरि लागौं कहरवा हो
डोली धर छिन बार ।
मिल लेवौं सखियां सहेलर हो
मिलौं कछु परिवार ।
दास कबीर गावै निरगुन हो
साधो करिले बिचार ।
नरम गरम सौदा करिलै हौ
आगे हाट ना बजार ।

aayo din goinekey ho mun hoth hulaas.
doliyaa uthhaawe bijaa bunwaa ho
jahan koi na humaar.
payaan thori laagon kaharwaa ho
doli dhar chhin baar.
mil leiboun sakhiyaan sahelur ho
miloun kachhu parivaar
das Kabir gaawe nirgun ho
saadho karileh bichaar
narum garum soudaa karileh ho
aage haat na bazaar.

Come is the day
to start for my Love's home.
My heart is gladdened
and mind is full of glee today.
In a palanquin was I carried
on the road to the deep forest.
I pleaded with the bearers,
"O brothers, do stop a moment
to let me bid a brief adieu
to my friends and relations."
Says Kabir—let me sing
the praise of the formless Supreme being!
O gentle folk! do quickly finish
all your give and take of earth,
there is no shop or market-place ahead.

NO. 33

अब मोहि ले चलु ननद के वीर अपने देसा ।
इन पांचन मिलि लूटीहुं
संग संग आहि विदेसा ।
गंग तीर मेरी खेती बारी
जमुना तीर खरिहाना ।
सात विरही मेरे नीपजे
पांचु मोर किसाना ।
कहे कबीर यह अकथ कथा है
कहत कही न जाई ।
सहज भाइ जिहि उपजै
ते रमि रहै समाई ।

ub mohi le chalu nanad ke bir apne deshaa.
in paanchan mili lutihum
sung sung aahi videshaa.
gung theer meri khethi baari
yamunaa theer kharihaanaa
saath birhi mere nipjey
paanchu more kisaanaa.
kahe Kabir yeh akath kathaa hei
kahath kahi na jaayi
sahaj vaahi jihi upajey
thei rami rahey samaayi.

Take me away to your land, my Love,
O my nanad's brother.
Together the five enemies here
have robbed me of every thing,
they never leave me alone.
All my lands are on the Ganges,
on the Yamuna the farmyard.
Five farm workers till my lands
and grow all the seven grains.
Says Kabir—untold is the story
it cannot be told in open.
I shall remain united with my Lord
whose love manifests easily.

NO. 34

आज मेरे घर पीतम आये ।
रहत रहत मैं अंगना बुहारूं
मोतियन आज पराये ।
चरन पधार तेज रस बरस
सब सावन बरसाऊं ।
बाट जगी मैं मंगल गाऊं
राग सूरत की जलाऊं ।
करुं आरती प्रेम निसि भरि
पल पल बनि बनि जाऊं ।
कहे कबीर धनि भाग हमारा
परमं पुरिस बर पाऊं ।

aaj mere ghur pitum aaye
rahath rahath mein unganaa buhaarun.
motiyan aaj paraaye.
charun padhaar thej rus baras
sub saaban barasaaun
baat jagi meine mangal gaaun
raag surath ki jalaaun.
karun aarathi prem nisi bhari
pul pul bani bani jaaun
kahe Kabir dhani vaag humaaraa
parum puris bur paaun.

Today will my Love come to my house
I am washing my courtyard again and again.
Bedecked I am with gems and gold.
When my Love will reach my house
it will glisten in His glow.
I shall light the lamp of love in me
and sing the welcome song to Him
I shall be with Him
all night through
basking in His bounteous love.
Says Kabir   what luck!
I shall wed tonight the Lord Supreme.

NO. 35

जीव महल में शिव पहुनवा कहाँ फिरत उनमाद रे ।
पहुंचा देवा कर लै सेवा रैन चली आवत रे ।
जुगन जुगन करै पतीछन साहब का दिल लागरे ।
सूझत-नाहिं परम सुख सागर बिना प्रेम बैराग रे ।
सरबन सुर बुझि साहब से पूरन परगट भाग रे ।
कहै कबीर सुनो भाग हमारा पाया अटल सोहाग रे ।

jiva mahal mein shiva pahunwaa
    kahaan phirath unmaad re.
pahunchaa devaa karle sebaa
    raein chali aawath re
jugan jugan karey pathichhan
    saahab kaa dil laag re.
sujhath naahin param sukh saagar
    vinaa prem vairaag re.
surbun sur bujhi saahaab se
    puran pargat bhaag re
kahe Kabir suno bhaag humaaraa
    paayaa atul sohaag re.

In your heart's chamber, dear
is your Lord the guest!
Where are you roaming and why
losing your wit and sense?
Engage yourself to serve the Lord,
unawares the dark night may engulf you!
For ages you are awaiting Him
do win His love and favour now.
Follow the path of love, non-attachment
to reach the ocean of delight.
Says Kabir—I now know
the import of His eternal message,
He himself brought it home to me.
What luck! I got
His tender touch of love.

NO. 36

सुख सागर को आयके मत जा रे प्यासा ।
अजहुँ समुझ नर बावरे
जम करत निरासा ।
निरमल नीर बहे तेरे पास
पीले स्वासों स्वांसा ।
मृग तृष्णा जल छाड़ बावरे
करो सुधा रस आसा ।
ध्रुव प्रहलाद सुकदेव पिया
और पिया रैदासा ।
प्रेमहि रस सदा मतवाला
एक प्रेम की आसा ।
कहै कबीर सुनो भाइ साधो
मिट गई भय की वासा ।

sukh saagar ko aayke muth jaa re pyaasaa.
ajahun samujh nar baabare
jum karath niraasaa.
nirmal neer bahe there pass
peele swanso swaasaa.
mrigathrusna jul chaad baabre
karo sudhaa rus ashaa
dhruv prahlad sukhdev piyaa
wor piyaa raidaasaa
premhi rus sadaa muthwaalla
ek prem ki aashaa.
kahe Kabir suno bhaai saadho
mit gayi vey ki baasaa.

Having come to the ocean of delight
do not go back in thirst.
Do not be stupid and indiscreet
beware, your life is in death's clutch.
Closeby flows the stream of pure water
drink to fill from that.
Do not run after mirages of earth
Seek the stream of love-devotion
be immersed in that.
Saints like Dhruv, Prahlad and Shukdev
as well as saint Raidasa
steeped themselves in the nectar of love
and realised Him; you too crave for that.
Says Kabir—"O, gentle folk listen
I have become fearless now!"

NO. 37

नाचूं रे मेरे मन मत्त होय
प्रेम की राग बजाय रैन दिन
सबद सुनै सब कोय ।
राहु केतु नवग्रह नाचै
जनम जनम आनंद होय ।
छापा तिलक लगाय बांस चढ़ि
हो रहा सब से न्यारा ।
सहस कला कर मन मोर नाचै
रीझैं सिरजन हारा ।

naachure mere mun math hoye.
prem ke raag bajaay rein deen
subda sunei sub koy.
raahu kethu nav grah naache
janma janma aanand hoy.
chhaapaa thilak lagaay baans chadhhi
ho rahaa subse nyaaraa
sahas kalaa kur mun mor naachey
rijhey sirjun haaraa.

My mind
do dance in delight
to the tune of the music of love
that swells eternally day and night
audible to one and all.
All the nine planets are dancing
for ages to the tune
steeped in untold glee.
The earth with its mountains, hills and dales
dances and dance all the living creatures
to the delight of the music,
and amidst their tears and laughter too
all men and women dance.
A few in the name of religion
try in vain to remain aloof
from the pervading music and dance.
Says Kabir—my mind steeped full in love
dances with abandon to the tune
The Lord Supreme beholds that
and is highly pleased!

NO. 38

सांई से लगन कठिन है भाई,
जैसे पपीहा प्यासा बूंद का पिया पिया रट लाई ।
प्यासे प्राण तड़फै दिन रैन
और नीर न भाई ।
जैसे मिरग सबद सनेही सबद सुनन को जाई
सबद सुनै और प्रान दान दें, तनिको नाहिं डराई ।
छोड़ो तन आपन को आसा, निर्भय है गुन गाई
कहत कबीर सुनो भाइ साधो नाहिं तो जनम नसाई ।

saainyin se legan kathhin hey vaai
jeise papihaa pyaasaa bund kaa
piyaa piyaa rata laayi
pyaase praan thudfe deen raiyen
wor neer na bhaayi
jyese mirga subad sanehi
subad sunun ko jaayyi
subad sune wor praan daan dey
thaniko naahin daraayi
chhodo thun aapan ko aashaa
nirvay whe guna gaayi
kahath Kabir suno bhaai saadho
naahin tho janam nasaayi.

It is indeed hard to win the Lord.
Like the rain bird, *papihaa*
flying in the lap of the gathering clouds,
calling loudly *piya piya*
waits for the *Swaati* rain to fall,
although tormented by acute thirst
does not crave any other water.
Like the deer fond of melody
drawn sans fear to the source of it
thereby losing his precious life
to the heartless hunter's callous gun.
If you hope to win the Lord
you have to snap the bonds of earth
of wealth and power and lust besides
forsake hope of your body
meditate Him and fearless sing His praise
Says Kabir—O gentle folk listen
or else you waste your life in vain.

NO. 39

निसि दिन खेलत रहि सखियन संग
मोहि बड़ा डर लागै ।
मोरे साहब की ऊंची अटारिया
चढ़त मोरि जियरां कांपै ।
जो सुख चाहै तो लज्या त्यागै
पिया से हिल मिल लागै ।
घूंघट खोल अंग भर भेटै
नैन आरती साजै ।
कहै कबीर सुनो सखि मोरी
प्रेम होय सो जानै ।
निज प्रीतम की आस नहीं है
नाहक काजर पारै ।

nisi deen khelat rahi sakhiyun sung
mohi badaa dur laagey
more saahub kaa unchi ataariyaa
chadhath mori jiyaraa kaampey
jo sukh chahey tho lajyaa thyaage
piyaa se hil mil laagey.
ghunghat khol ung bhur bhete
nayen aarati saajey.
kahe Kabir suno sakhi mori
prem hoy so jaaney
nija pritum ki aash naahin hey
naahuk kaajar paarey.

With my friends and companions
I was playing all day and night.
Closeby was my Love's tall mansion
the apex room is where he lives.
To ascend to it
I shivered in fear and shame
and wondered how
I could have union with my Love
unless I shed my bashfulness,
uncovered my face, made body bare
and clasped and clung to Him
and in the light of my eyes
offered *aarati* to the Lord.
Says Kabir—O my friend listen!
she alone can comprehend
if her love for Him is true and deep
but if not so
futile will be all her make up.

NO. 40

दुलहिन अंगिया काहे न धोवाई ।
बालापन की मैली अंगिया विषय दाग परि जाई
बिन धोये पिया रीझत नाहिं सेज से देत गिराई ।
सुमिरन ध्यान के साबुन करिलै सत नाम दरियायी
दुविधा के भेद खोल बहुरिया मन के मैल धोबाई ।
चेत करो तिन पन बीते, अब तो गवन नगिचाई
पालनहार द्वार है ठाढ़े अब काहे पछिताई
कहत कबीर सुनोरि बहुरिया चित अंजन दे आई ।

dulahin angiyaa kaahe na dhobaayi
baala pun ki mailee angiyaa
visay daag pari jaayi
bin dhoeye piyaa rijhath naahin
shej se det giraayi
sumirun dhyaan ke saabun kariley
suth naam dariyaayi
dubidhaa ke bhed khol bohuriya
mun ke maiyl dhobaayi,
cheth karo thin pun bithey
ub tho gaban nagichaayi
paalan haar dwar hei thhadeh
ub kaahe pachhithaayi
kahat Kabir sunori bohuriyaa
chith anjan dey aayi.

O gentle lady,
Why do you not wash your blouse?
Since childhood days it is not washed,
the stains of earthly urges and deeds
are showing their ugly face on it.
Your Love will not like that at all
will push you from the bed in disgust.
With the soap of meditation
and His Name as pure water
with steadfast faith you wash it well
and shed your mind's strife
the stains will disappear.
Beware three fourths of your life is gone
the end of your days is near at hand.
Says Kabir—the Lord is at your door
clean up your wisdom's eye young maiden
do not be shy any more
behold Him face to face.

NO. 41

तिमिर सांझ का गहरा आवे
छावे प्रेम तन मन में ।
पछिम दिस का खिड़की खोलो
डूबहु प्रेम गनन में ।
चेत कमल दल रस पियो रे
लहर लेहु या तन में ।
संख घंटा सहनाई बाजै
शोभा सिंध महल में ।
कहै कबीर सुनो भाइ साधो
अमर साहब लख घट में ।

thimbir saanjh kaa gaheraa aawey
chaawe prem thun mun mein.
pachhim dis kaa khidki kholo
dubahu prem gagan mein.
cheth kambal dul rus piyo re
lahar lehu yaa thun mein
sankh ghantaa sahnaai baaje
shovaa sindh mahal mein.
kahe Kabir suno bhaai saadho
amar saahab lukh ghutmein.

Evening shadows darken deep
the body and mind get steeped in love.
Open the western window and see
the surging sea of love in the sky.
Take a dip in that
and drink the honey of love
overflowing from the lotus of your heart,
feel it surge through your body,
harken the peal of bells and conch
from the temple in your heart.
Says Kabir—O gentle soul behold
the Lord is within you!

NO. 42

मन मस्त हुआ तब क्यूं बोले ।
हीरा पाय गांठ गंठियायो, बार बार वाको क्यूं खोले ।
हलकी थी तब चढ़ी तराजू, पूरी भई तब क्यूं तोले ।
सुरत कलारी भइ मतवारी, मदवा पी गइ बिन तोले ।
हंसा पाये मानसरोवर, ताल तलेंया क्यूं डोले ।
तेरा साहब हें घट माहिं, बाहर नैना क्यूं खोलै ।
कहे कबीर सुनो भाइ साधो, साहब मिल गये तिल ओले ।

mun musth huaa thub kuyon bole?
hiraa paaye gaanthh gunthiyaayo
baar baar wah ko kyun khole.
hulki thhee thub chaddhi tharaaju
puri vayi thub kyun thoule?
surath kalaari vayi muthwaari
mudwa peegayi bin thoule.
hunsa paaye maan sarobur
taal thaleyaa kyun doley
theraa saahub hei ghut maahi
baahaar nainaa kyun khole
kahe Kabir suno bhaai saadho
saahab mil gaye thil oule.

When my mind overflows with love
why need I open my lips?
I have gained the precious Diamond
and wrapped it in my cloth,
why need I unwrap it again and again?
With a little load the pan went up
when the load is full why need I weigh?
The vendor became himself drunk
drinking sans limit from his vat.
The swan has reached the mountain lake
why should she hanker puddles and holes?
Your Lord is within you, my dear
Why need you seek Him here and there?
Says Kabir—O gentle folk listen!
like the oil in the oilseed
the Lord is within you indeed!

NO. 43

ये अंखियां अलसानी
पिया हो सेज चलो ।
खंबा पकरि पतंग अस डोले
ना बोलै मधुर बानी ।
फूलन सेज बिछायि जो राख्यो
पिया बिना कुम्हलानी ।
धीरे ठांव धरो पलंग पर
जागत ननद जिठानी ।
कहत कबीर सुनो भाइ साधो
लोक लाज बिछलानी ।

yea aankhiyaan alsaani
piyaa ho sej chalo.
khambaa pakari patung us dolei
naa boley madhur baani
phulan sej bichhaayi jo raakhyo
piyaa binaa kumhlaani
dhire thhaaon dharo palungaa per
jaaguth nanad jethhaani
kahat Kabir suno bhaayi saadho
lok laaj bichhlaani.

My eyes are drooping with sleep, my Love
come, let us go to bed.
Love-lorn my body quivers like the butterfly
I cannot utter two sweet words.
The flowers I decked by bed with
are getting stale and drying up.
Do step cautiously on to the bed, my Love
my sister and aunt are still awake!
Says Kabir—O gentle folk listen,
for fear of others' ridicule
I am shy of uniting with my Love!

NO. 44

अमृत बरसै हीरा निपजाये
घंट पड़े टकसाल ।
कबीर जुलाहा पाया पारस
अनभै उतरिया पार ।
कबीर हरि रस यूं पिया
बाकी रही न ताकी ।
पाका कलश कुम्हार का
बहुरि न चढ़ाई चाकी ।

amrit varase hiraa nipjaaye
ghanta pade taksaal
Kabir jullaha paaya paaras
unbhey uthariyaa paar.
Kabir hari rus yun piyaa
baaki rahi na thaaki
paakaa kalus kumhaar ka
bohuri na chaddhayi chaaki.

Nectar rained down from the sky
and bells pealed out in the temple
when Kabir gained his precious Touch-stone
Now he can cross
the earthly ocean
without fear of any kind.
Kabir is drunk with the nectar of love.
He drank to his fill and over more
and now he is quite confident
that like the well-baked earthen pot
he will not come to the wheel
of life and death again.

NO. 45

भीजै चुनरिया प्रेम रस बूंदन ।
आरति साज कै चलि सुहागन
पिया अपने को ढूंढन ।
काहे की तोरी बनी चुनरिया
काहे के लागे चारों फूंदन ।
पांच तत्त की बनी चुनरिया
नाम के लागे फूंदन ।
चढ़िगै महल खुलगई किंबरिया
दास कबीर लागै झूलन ।

vijey chunariyaa prem rus bundun.
aarati saaj kei chali suhaagin
piyaa apne ko ddhundan.
kaaheki thori bani chunariyaa
kaaheko laagey chaaron phoondun
paanch thathki bani chunariyaa
naam ke laagey phoondun.
chaddhigey mahal khulgayi kibariyaa
daas Kabir laagey jhoolan.

Soaked is the body and mind of the beloved
in deep love of the Lord
her *saari* too is soaked in it.
With the tray of *aarati* in her hand
she is out to meet her Love.
Of what is your *saari* made, O maiden
and what does make you frolicsome?
Says Kabir—O gentle folk listen,
my *saari* is made of the elements five
my Love's Name potion gladdens me
and when I went up the steps of His mansion
lo! the door opened out on to me
I felt like swaying in the swing!

NO. 46

जागु पियारी अब का सोवै
रैन गई दिन काहेको खोवै ।
जिन जागा तिन मानिक पाया
तै बौरी सब सोये गंबाया ।
पिया तेरे चतुर तू मूरख नारी
कबहुं न पिया की सेज सँवारी ।
तैं बौरी बौरा पन कीन्है
भर जोवन आपन पिया न चीन्है ।
जाग देख पिया सेज न तेरे
तोहि छोड़ उठ गये सवेरे ।
कहे कबीर सोइ धुन जागे
सबद बान अंतर लागे ।

jaagu piyaari ub kya sobey
raiyn gayi deen kaaheko khobey?
jin jaagaa theen maanik paaya
thein bouri sub soye gumbaayaa
piyaa there chathur thu murakh naari
kabahun na piyaaki sej samvari
thein bouri bouraa pun kinhe
bhur jovan aapan piyaa na chinhey
jaag dekh piyaa sej na there
thohi chhod uthh gaye sabere.
kahe Kabir soyi dhun jaagey
subad baan anthar laagey.

Maiden do wake up from your slumber
whole of the night you have slept like a log
why should you lose the day too sleeping?
The alert and wakeful wins the Gem
In slumber you have missed the chance.
Clever is your Love, you little fool
never you bedecked your bed for Him.
Bereft of your cleverness
You failed to know your Love in your youth
Wake up and see your Love is gone
leaving you in the bed before dawn.
Says Kabir—do listen to the call of His flute
the eternal music will touch your heart!

NO. 47

नैना उंतरि आव तूं
ज्यौ हौं नैन झंपेउं ।
ना हौं देखौं और कूँ
ना तुम देखन देउं ।
कबीर रेख सिंदूर की,
काजर दिया न जाइ ।
नैनू रमैया रमि रह्या,
दूजा कहँ समाइ ।
मन परतीत न प्रेम रस,
ना इत तन में ढंग ।
क्या जानै उस पीवसू,
कैसे रहसी रंग ।

nainaa unthari aawa thun
jyo houn nein jhumpeun
naa houn dekhoun wor kuun
naa thujh dekhun deun.
Kabir rekh sindur kee
kaajar diyaa na jaayi
neinu ramayaa rami rahyaa
dujaa kaahan samaayi
mun partheeth na prem rus
naa eeth thun mein dhhung
kyaa jaaney oos peeb suun
keise rahasi rung.

O Love, do come
this once inside my eye
I shall at once drop the lids,
so I alone shall see You there
and me alone You will see.
Says Kabir, in the vermilion box
You cannot put dark *Kaajar*.
My Love, Lord Raam, occupies my eye
none else can I lodge there.
I fear my love is neither deep
nor have I a beauteous face,
I do not know how my dear Love
will like to take to me.

NO. 48

सखियां हम हुं भई बलमासी ।
आयो जोबन बिरह सतायो
अब मैं ज्ञान गली अठिलाती ।
ज्ञान गली में खबर मिलि गई
हमैं मिली पिया की पाती ।
वा पाती में अगम संदेसा
अब हम मरन को ना डराती ।
कहत कबीर सुनो भाइ प्यारे
वर पाये अविनासी ।

sakhiyaan hum hun bhayee bulmaasi
aayo joban viraha sataayo
ub mein gyaan gali athilaathi
gyaan gali mein khavur mili gayee
humein milee piyaa ki paathi
waa paathi mein agum sundeshaa
ub hum marun ko na daaraathi.
kahat Kabir suno bhaai pyaare
vur paaye avinaasi.

O my friends! for want of my Love
acute is my pain of yearning.
My youth is making it still more so
the pang of it is unbearable.
I was seeking in the lanes of knowledge
the way to endure the agony.
Lo! I got it there,
my Love Himself did prescribe
the miracle cure!
I am no more dreading death, my friends!
Says Kabir—O dear friends do listen,
I am going to wed my Love
the Eternal Lord.

NO. 49

आइ न सकूं तुझ पे, सकूं न तुझ बुलाई ।
ज़ियरा यों ही लेहुंगे, विरह तपाइ तपाई ।
यह तन जालौ राख करि, ज्यूं धुंवा जाइ सरग्गि ।
मति ते राम दया करें, बरसि बुझावै अग्गि ।
यह तन जालौं मसि करौं, लिखूं राम का नांव ।
लिखनी करैं करंक की, लिखि लिखि राम पठाउं ।
इस तन का दीवा करौं, बाती मेलूं जीव ।
लोही सींचे तेल ज्यूं, कब मुख देखौं पीव ।
कै बिरहिन कूं मीच दे, कै आप दिखलाइ ।
आठ पहर का दझना, मौ पें सह्या न जाइ ।

aayi na sakun thuj pey
sakun na thujh bulaayi.
jiyaraa yonhi lehunge
virah thapaayi thapaayi.
yah thun jaalun raakh karun
jyu dhuaan jaayi saraggi
mathi they raam dayaa karey
varasi bujhaaweh aaggi
yah thun jaalun masi karun
likhun raam kaa naam.
likhani karaun karank ki
likhi likhi raam pathhaaun
ish thun kaa divaa karun
baathi melyun jib
lohi sinche thel jyun
kub mukh dekhun peeb.
keyy virahin kuun meech de
keyy aap dikhlaayi
aathh paharkaa dujhnaa
mou pay sahyaa na jaayi.

I am not able to come to You
nor can make You come to me.
The pang of separation pains me so
I cannot live with it.
I shall burn my body to ash
its smoke will rise to heaven
Raam, my Love, will notice that
and shower His blessing,
so the fire will choke and quench.
I shall burn my body, make ink with the ash
and with my bone as pen shall I write
my Love Raam's name
and send the message of my sorrow to Him.
Of my body I shall make a lamp
add my blood as oil in it
my life I shall put as wick there
and in the light of the lamp
see my Love's winsome face.
My Love, my Lord do show Your face
or give me death and let me die.
I cannot endure
the pang of separation any more.

NO. 50

हरि मेरा पीव भाई हरि मेरा पीव
हरि बिन रह न सकै मेरा जीव ।
हरि मेरा पीव में हरि की बहुरिया
राम बड़े में छुटकि लहुरिया ।
किया स्यंगार मिलन के ताइ
काहे ना मिले राजा राम गुसांई ।
अबकी बेर मिलन जो पावूं
कहे कबीर भौ जल नहिं आऊं ।

hari meraa peeb vaayi hari meraa peeb.
hari bin rah na sakei meraa jeeb.
hari meera peeb mein hariki bahuriyaa
raam bade mein chhutaki lahuriyaa.
kiyaa singaar milun ki thaayi
kaahe na miley raaja raam gusaainyi
ub ki ber milun jo paaum
kahe Kabir vow jul naahin aaun.

The Lord is my Love, O friend
Lord Hari is my Love
without Him I cannot live a moment.
Raja Rama is my Love
and I am His consort,
He is so great, I am so small a fry!
But, I have bedecked myself
for our meeting.
Where has He gone?
Why is He tarrying?
Says Kabir—if I get my Love this time
never shall I come earthwards again.

NO. 51

संतो अंधा धुंधि अंधियारा ।
इसी घट अंदर बाग बगीचा
इसी में सिरजनहारा ।
इसी घट भीतर सात समुंदर
इसी में नौ लख तारा ।
इसी घट अंदर हीरा मोती
इसी में परखन हारा ।
इसी घट अंदर अनहद बाजा
इसी में उठत फुवारा ।
कहै कबीर सुनो भाइ साधो
यहि है गुरू हमारा ।

santo andaadhundi andhiyaaraa.
isi ghut undur baag bagichaa
isi mein sirjun haaraa.
isi ghut bhithar saat samandur
isi mein nau lukh tharaa
isi ghut undur heera mothi
isi mein parkhan haaraa.
isi ghut undur unhud baajaa
isi mein uthhath phuwaaraa.
kahe Kabir suno bhaai saadho
yahi hei guru humaaraa.

O gentle folk!
why are you groping in the dark?
In this body is the flower garden
the benign Creator stays here.
All the seven seas are here
and all the myriad stars.
In this body are all the gems
and also the unknown Tester.
Here the Eternal music swells
and surge the fountains of life.
Says Kabir—listen O gentle folk!
this is my Guru who guides me.

NO. 52

नैहरवा हमका नहिं भावै ।
सांई की नगरी परम अति सुंदर
जहँ कोइ जाइ न आवै ।
चांद सुरज जहँ पवन न पानी
को संदेस पहुंचावै ।
दरद यह सांइ को सुनावै ।
आगे चले पंथ नहिं सूझै
पीछे दोस लगावै ।
किहि विधि सुसरे जाउं मोरि सजनी,
बिरह जोर जलावै ।
विषय रस नाच नचावै,
बिन सतगुरू अपना नहिं कोई
जो यह राह बतावै ।
कहत कबीर सुनो भाइ साधो
सुपने न प्रीतम पावै
तपन यह तन की बुझावै ।

neihurwaa humkaa naahin vaawe
saayin ki nagari param athee sunder
jahaan jaay koyi na aawe.
chaand suraj jahan pavan na paani
ko sundesaa pahunchaawe
dard yaha saayin ko sunaawe.
aage chale panth naahin sujhe
pichhey dosh lagaawe
kihi bidhi susarey jaaun mori sajani
birah jor jalaawe
bisei rus naatch nachaawe.
bin suthguru apanaa naahin koyi
jo yah raaha bathaawe
kahath Kabir suno bhaai saadho
supne na preethum paawe
thapan yaha thunki bujhaawe.

I do not relish my stay with parents,
the city of my Love is so lovely
I wish to go there.
None comes back from that blissful land,
sun nor moon, water nor wind exist there.
Who will carry the message of my pain
to my Love?
Acute is my agony for want of Him
the earthly urges bind me hands and feet
I yearn too much for my Love's palace
but the path ahead is full of hurdles,
the messenger will rebuke me.
None other than my *Guru*
knows the correct route.
He alone can help if he likes.
Says Kabir—O gentle folk listen!
You cannot get your Love in dream
to allay your anguish.

NO. 53

जौ पैं पियके मन नाहि भायै
तो का परोसनि कै दुलरायै ।
कहा चूड़ा पायल झमकायै
कहा भयै बिछुवा ठनकायै ।
कहा काजर सिंदूर कै दियै
सोलह सिंगार कहा भये किये ।
अंजन मंजन करै ठगौरी
का पचि मरै ठगौरी बौरी ।
जो पतिब्रता है नारी
कैसेहि रहो सो पियहि पियारी ।
तन मन जीवन सौंपि सरीरा
ताहि सोहागन कहै कबीरा ।

jo pey piyake mun naahi vaaye
tho kyaa parosani key dularaayeh.
kahaa churaa paayal jhamkaayea
kahaa vaye bichhua thhanakaaye.
kahaa kaajar sindur kei diye
solah singaar kahaa vaye kiye.
anjan munjan karei thhagouri
kaa pachi mare thhagouri bouri
jo pey pathibrathaa whey naari
keise hi raho so piyahi piyaree.
tun mun jibun soumpi sariraa
thahi sohagin kahe Kabiraa.

If you cannot win the love of the Lord
what if you can lord over your neighbour?
What is the good of dressing your hair
and donning your feet with jingling jewellery?
What is the value of all your make up
with kajar to your eyelids
and vermilion to your forehead
and all the efforts to deck yourself
if you are not loyal in your love?
It is all a self deception
and does not touch the Lord at all.
Says Kabir—if you can surrender
your body, mind and heart to the Lord
and remain loyal in love to Him,
sans make up and ornaments
you will win His favour
in whatever state you be!

NO. 54

चलो सखि जाइय तहाँ जहाँ गये पाइये परमानंद
यह मन आमन दूमना मेरे तन छीजै नित जाइ
चिंतामणि चित चौरियो तथे कछु न सुहाइ ।
सुनि सखी सुपने की गति ऐसी हरि आये हम पास
सोवतहि जु जगाइया जागत भये उदास ।
चल सखी बिलम न कीजिए जब लगि सांस सरीर
मिलि रहिये जगनाथ सूं यूं कहै दास कबीर ।

chalo sakhi jaayiye thahaan
jaahaan gaye paayiye parammaanund.
yaha mun aamun dumunaa mere
thun chhije nitha jaayi.
chyntamani chith chouriyeo
thathey kachhu na suhaayi.
suni sakhi supaneki gathi eysi
hari aaye hum paas
sobuth hi ju jagaayiyaa
jaagath vaye udaas.
chal sakhi bilum na kijiyea
jub lug saans sarir
mili rahiyea jagannathh suun
yun kahe daas Kabir.

O my friend let us go there
where we shall get
the highest bliss of happiness!
My mind is so very unstable
sometimes it helps or else it hinders
my body is wasting day to day.
My Lord has stolen my mind and heart
so I am so restless.
O my friend listen!
in dream did my Lord come to me
and woke me up from sleep
but alas! on my waking
He became callous and cold.
Says Kabir—let us this now go there
for so long I live I want to be
as close I can to my Lord!

NO. 55

सांई मेरे साजि दई एक डोली
हसत लोग अरू मैं तैं बोली ।
इक झंझर सम सूत खटोला
त्रिस्ना भाव चहूँ दिसि डोला ।
पांच कहार का मरम न जाना
एकै कहा एकै नहिं माना ।
भूभर धाम उहार न छावा
नैहरि जात बहु दुखु पावा ।
कहै कबीर बर दुखु सहिये
राम प्रीति करि संग रहिये ।

saayin mere saaji dayi ek doli,
hasuth log aru mey thei boli.
ik jhanjhar sum sut khatolaa
thrisnaa vaaw chahudisi dolaa.
paanch kahar kaa marum na jaanaa
ekei kahaa ekei nahi maanaa.
vubhar ghaam uhaar na chhawaa
neihari jaath bahu dukh paawaa.
kahe Kabir bur dukhu sahiye
raam priti kari sung rahiye.

My Lord arranged a palanquin
for me to visit my father's house.
People made fun of me and talked this and that.
In the palanquin was a frail bedstead
as frail as made of brittle yarn
it swayed to the urges of the world.
Five were the palanquin bearers
each unknowing and wild in nature
none listened to the words of the other.
The palanquin did not have even a screen
to protect from the hot winds blowing
the journey to father's house was painful.
Says Kabir—it is far better to love Lord Raam
and stay with Him
and court the pain and sorrow thereof
than live with the griefs of the father's house.

NO. 56

चली मैं खोज में पिया की,
मिटी नहीं सोच यह जिया की ।
रहे नित पास ही मेरे
ना पाऊं यार को हेरे ।
बिकल चहुँ ओर को धाऊं
तबहुँ नहिं कंत को पाऊं ।
धरों केहि भांति से धीरा,
गये गिर हाथ से हीरा ।
कटी जब नैन की झांई,
लख्यो तब गगन में सांई ।
कबीर सबद कहि त्रासा
नयन में यार को बासा ।

chali mein khoj mein piyaaki
miti naahin soch yaha jiyaaki.
rahe neeth pass hi mere
naa paaun yaar ko herey
bikal chaahun wor ko dhaayun
thabahi naahin kunt ko paaun.
dharon kehi vanthi se dhiraa
gaye gir hath se heera
kati jub nain ki jhaayin
lakhyo thub gagan mein saaiyin
Kabir subad kahi thraasaa
nayan mein yaar ko baasaa.

I am out in search of my Love,
for want of Him I am always restless
He, my Love, is so near me
but my eyes fail to notice.
Distraught I wander here and there
I do not get my consort anywhere.
If somehow I steady my mind
I feel I have dropped
the Diamond somewhere.
When the shadow was removed from my eye
I saw my Love in the sky.
Says Kabir—my Love resides in my eye!

NO. 57

आई गवनवा की सारी उमरि अबहि मोरी बारी ।
साज समाज पिया लै आये और कहरवा चारी
बाम्हन बेदरदी अंचरा पकरिकै जोरत गंठिया हमारी ।
सखि सब पारत गारी ।
बिधि गति बाम कछु समझ परतना बैरी भयि महतारी
रोय रोय अंखियां मोरि पोछत घर से देत निकारी ।
भई सब को हम भारी ।
गौन कराय पिया लै चले इत उत बाट निहारी
छूटत नगरी गांव से नाता छूटे महल अटारी ।
करम गति टारे ना टारी ।
नदिया किनारे बलम मोर रसिया, दीन घूंघट पट टारी
थर थराय तनु कांपन लागे, काहु न देखि हमारी,
पिया लै आये गौहारी ।

aayi.gawanwa ki saari
umri abahi mori baari.
saaj sumaaj piyaa ley aaye
wor kaharwaa chaari.
baamhun beddrdi anchiraa pakarike
jorath gunthiyaa humaari
sakhi sub paarath gaari.
bidhi gathi baam kachhu samajhi parathi na
bairee vaye mahathaari.
roy roy ankhinyaa mori poçhhath
ghur se deth nikaari.
vayi subko hum bhaari.
goun karaay piyaa le chalei
it uth baat nihari
chhutath nagari gaon se naathaa
chhute mahul ataari.
karm gathi taare na taari.
nadiyaa kinaare balam mor rasiyaa
deen ghunghat pat taari
thhar thhuraay thanu kaampun laage
kaahu na dekhi humaari
piyaa le aaye gouhaari.

My Love has brought me the farewell *saari*
O friends! it is time for me
to bid the last adieu and depart for good!
All things for the farewell has He brought
and four carriers too
to bear my body away.
As they don me the farewell *saari*
the heartless Brahmin tugs at it
to tie the knot
that annoys my friends—they rebuke him.
I do not know why my mother and matrons
have suddenly turned hostile to me.
Though they themselves weep
as they brush my tears away
together they bear my body
in such a rough and tumble way
it is hard to comprehend why.
For our wedding
my Love led the carriers to the river side
viewing on the way the village huts
and city mansions of many hues
and tearing all my links with them.
None can alter the outcome of my deeds!
At the river the stretcher was lowered
my Love bent over me
and smiling tenderly
lifted the veil from my face!
I quaked in the urge of love and fear.
None else was there
My Love smiled again
and picked me up in a tender hug!

NO. 58

अविनासी दूल्हा का मिलेहै भक्तन के रछपाल।
जल उपजी जलही सों नेहा रटत पिआस पिआस
मैं ठाढ़ी बिरहिन मग जोउं प्रियतम तुम्हरी आस ।
छोड़े गेह नेह लगि तुम सों भई चरन लव लीन
तालावेलि होति घर भीतर जैसे जल बिन मीन ।
दिवस न भूख रैन नहिं निद्रा घर अंगना न सुहाय
सेजरियां बैरिन भइ हमको जागत रैन विहाय ।
हमतो तुमरी दासी सजना तुम हमरे भरतार
दीनदयाल दया करि आओ समरथ सिरजनहार ।
कै हम प्रान तजति है प्यारे कै अपन कर लेव
दास कबीर बिरह अति बाढ़वे हम को दरसन देव ।

avinaashi dulhaa ka milihey
vakathanke rachhpaal.
jul upaji jul hi soun nehaa
ratath piyaas piyaas
mein thhaadi virahin muga joun
priyathum thumhaari aash.
chhode geha neha laagi thumha soun
bhayi charun lava leen,
thala beli hoth ghur bhithar
jeise jul bin min.
dibas na bhukh reyen nahi nidraa
ghur anganaa na suhaay,
sejaria beirin bhayi humko
jaagath reyen bihaay.
humtho thumhari daasi sajanaa
thum hum re varthaar
deen dayaal dayaa kari aayo
sumruth sirjun haar.
kei hum praan thajathi hei pyaare
kei apanaa kur lev.
daas Kabir virah athi baadhbey
hum ko darsun deb.

O my Eternal Love! Protector of devotees!
When shall I meet You?
As fish though born of water
and living in it always
cries for water to quench his thirst
so I am always hankering for You
being unable to attain You, my Love.
Forsaking home I am seeking You
restless like fish out of water.
I do not relish any food
nor do I sleep at night
At home I do not feel at home,
my bed I feel as bed of thorns.
I am Your slave, You are my consort,
O, Omnipotent Creator
have mercy on me, my Love
do take me in Your arms
or else I shall succumb.
Says Kabir—too acute is my agony
O Lord, do come, do not tarry.

NO. 59

अंखियां तो छाई परी
पंथ निहारि निहारि ।
जीहड़ियां छाला परया
नाम पुकारि पुकारि।
बिरह कमंडल कर लिये
बैरागी दो नैन ।
मांगे दरस मधूकरी
छकै रहै दिन रैन ।
सब रंग तांति रबाब तन,
बिरह बजावै नित ।
और न कोई सुनि सकै,
कै सांई के चित ।

ankhiyaan tho chhaayi pari
punth nihaari nihaari
jihadiyaa chaalaa parayaa
naam pukaari pukaari,
virah kamandal kur liye
vairaagi do nainyn,
maage darash madhukari
chhakei rahei deen reiyn.
sub rung thaanthi ravaw thun
virah bajaawe nith,
wor na koyi suni sakey
ke saayin ke chith.

Watching always for my Lord
a shadow screen has covered my eyes
my tongue is raw and abraded
chanting His name always.
With the pang of separation
as my begging bowl
with vacant look in my eyes
I am begging for a glimpse of Him
waiting and watching for Him always.
The pang of separation is wailing
in the veena of my heart.
It is inaudible to all others
only the Lord and I hear the strain.

NO. 60

नैहर में दाग लगाय आइ चुनरी ।
वो रंग रेजवा कै मरम न जानै
नाहिं मिलै धोबिया कवन करै उजरी ।
तन की कूंडी ग्यान का सउँदन
साबुन महँग बिकाय या नगरी ।
पहिरि ओढ़ि कै चली ससुरिया
गैवां के लोग कहैं बड़ी फुहरी ।
कहत कबीर सुनो भाइ साधो
बिन सतगुर कबहुं नहिं सुधरी ।

neihar mein daag laggay aayi chunri
wo rung rajwaa kei marum na jaanei
naahi mile dhobiyaa kawan karei ujaree?
thun ke koondi gyaan kaa saundun
saabun mahung vikaay yaa nagari.
pahari odhi kei chali sasuriyaa
gaivan ke log kahei badi phuhari.
kahath Kabir suno bhai saadho
vin sathguru kavahun nahi sudhri.

In my *saari* did I sustain
stains in my father's house.
The colour-artist did not know
how to set it right
nor was there a washerman
to wash the *saari* bright.
Little was my store of knowledge
and soap was selling dear too.
No help was there but to go
in the self-same stained *saari*
to my in-law's house.
People there whispered I was careless, silly.
Says Kabir—O gentle folk listen,
without *Sathguru's* help the stains cannot go.

NO. 61

पिया मोर जागे मैं कैसे सोई री ।
पांच सखी मेरे संग की सहेली
उन रंग रंगी पिया रंग ना मिली री ।
सास सयानी ननद दौंरानी
उन इर इरी पिया सार न जानी री ।
द्वादस पर सेज बिछानी
चढ़ न सकौं मेरी लाज लजानी री ।
रात दिवस मोहि कूका मारै
मैं न सुना रचि रही संग जानी री ।
कहे कबीर सुन सखी सयानी
बिन सतगुरू पिया मिलै न मिलानी री ।

piyaa mor jaagey mein keise soyee ri?
paanch sakhi mere sung ki saheli
uun rung rungi
piyaa rung na mili ri
saas sayaani nanad deworaani
uun dur dari piyaa saar na jaani ri
dwadus uper sej bichhaani
chadhh na sakoun meri laaj lajaani ri,
raath divus mohi kukaa maarey
mein na sunaa rachi rahi sung jaani ri,
kahe Kabir suun sakhi sayaani
vin suthguru piyaa miley na milaani ri.

My Love is awake now can I sleep?
Five are my constant friends
and being always under their sway
I cannot pay heed to my Love
and so I fail to get His favour.
For fear of my in-laws and sisters
I cannot come close to my Love
to know His mind.
In the apex room twelve stories up
is laid my Love's bed
I am ashamed and unable to go up there
to be near Him.
The pang of separation is pinching me
it pains me night and day.
I have not heard His voice as yet
nor enjoyed His company.
Says Kabir—O friends know it for certain
without the kind Guru's aid
none can hope to win His love.

NO. 62

बहुत दिनन की जोवती, बाट तुम्हारी राम ।
जिय तरसे तुझ मिलनकूं, मनि नाहीं बिसराम ।
बिरहिन उठै भी पड़ै, दरसन कारनि राम ।
मूवा पाछै देहुगै, सो दरसन केहि काम ।
मूवा पाछे जनि मिलै, कहै कबीरा राम ।
पथर घाटा लोह सब, पारस कौनो काम ।
बासरि सुख न रैनि सुख, ना सुख सुपने माहिं ।
कबीर बिछूटिया राम सूं, ना सुख धूप न छाँहि ।

bohut dinun ki jovti
baat thumhaari Raam
jiya tharase thujh milan kuun
mani naahin visraam
virahin uthhey vi padey
darasun kaarani Raam
muvaa paachhe dehugey
so darsun kehi kaam?
muvaa paachhe jani miley
kahe Kabiraa Raam
pathar ghaataa loha sub
paaras kouno kaam?
baasuri sukh naa reinee sukh
naa sukh supiney maahin.
Kabir bichhutiyaa Raam suun
naa sukh dhup naa chaahin.

O Raam, my Love!
For many and many a day
have I been waiting and pining for You.
For meeting You I am so restless,
I have no peace of mind
the pang of separation pains me so
I cannot even stand erect
pining for just a glimpse of You.
Says Kabir—O Raam! if I shall meet You
only after my death
like getting the touch-stone
after iron has become stone in earth,
what is the use of that?
Ununited with You, my Love
I am distraught during day and night
in shade and sunshine
and even in dream.

NO. 63

मैं सासनै पीब गौहानि आई
सांई संग साध नहिं पूगी गयो जोबन सुपना की नाईं ।
पंच जना मिलि मंडप छायो तीन जना मिलि लगन लिखाई ।
सखी सहेली मंगल गावैं सुख दुख माथे हलदि चढ़ाई ।
नाना रंग भांवरि फेरी गांठ जोरि बैठे पतिताई ।
पूरि सुहांग भयो बिन दूलह चौक के रंग धरयो सगो भाई ।
अपने पुरिस मुख कबहु न देख्या सति होति समझि समझाई ।
कहै कबीर हुं सर रचि मरिहूं तिरौं कंत लै तूर बजाई ।

mein saasnei peeb gouhaani aayi
saayin sung saadh nahi puugi
gayo jobun suupnaa ki naayi
paanch janaa mili mandup chhayo
theen janaa mili lagan likhaayi
sakhi saheli mangul gaawen
sukh dukh maathe huldi chadhaayi.
naanaa rung vaambri pheri
gaanthh jori baitthe pathithaayi.
poori suhaag vayo bin dullaah
chouk kei rungi dharayo sagou bhaayi.
apne puris mukh kabahun na dekhyaa
sati hoth samajhi samajhaayi.
kahe Kabir hum sur rachi marihum
thirou kunth le thur bajaayi.

I went to my father-in-law's house
to be near my Spouse
Though my youth was fading like a dream
I had not met my Love so long!
Five men had thatched the wedding altar
three had fixed the auspicious hour
my friends sang the wedding song
and applied turmeric to my head
I went round and round the sacred fire
and sat down with my apron tied.
Thus in absence of my Spouse
was my wedding done.
My brother acted as the guardian
but I had not seen
the face of my Spouse till then.
Only a chaste and loyal woman
can grasp the ache of that.
Says Kabir—I shall drown myself
in the lake; and crossing to the other shore
march ahead hand in hand with my Spouse
playing the trumpet together with Him..

NO. 64

कियो सिंगार मिलन की ताई
हरि न मिले जग जीवन गुसांई ।
हरि मेरो पिया हौं हरि की बहुरिया
राम बड़े मैं तनक लहुरिया ।
धनि पिया एकै संग बसेरा
सेज एक पै मिलन दुहेरा ।
धन सुहागिन जो पिया भावै
कहै कबीर फिर जनमि न आवै ।

kiyo singaar milan ki thaayi
hari na mile jaga jibun gusaain.
hari mero piyaa houn hariki bahuriyaa
Raam bade mein thanuk lahuriyaa.
dhani piyaa ek sung baseraa
sej ek pei milun duheraa
dhann suhaagin jo piyaa vaawe
kahe Kabir phir janami na aawe.

I bedecked myself for meeting my Love
alas, I could not find Him.
The Lord of the Universe
He is my Love and I am His consort.
Raam is great, I am too small a being.
Glory to her who lives with Him
and shares His bed.
Lucky is she who is loved by the Spouse.
Says Kabir—she gains salvation
has no rebirth.

NO. 65

अकथ कहानी प्रेम की, कछु कही न जाइ
गूंगे केरी सरकरा, बैठे मुसकाइ ।
भौमि बिना और बीज बिन, तरवर एक भई
अनंत फल प्रकासिया, गुरू दिया बताई ।
मन थिर वैसे बिचारिया, रामहि ल्यो लाइ,
झूठी मन में विस्तरि, सब थोथी बाइ ।
कहै कबीर सकति कछु नाहिं,
गुरू भया सहाई ।
आवन जानी मिट गई,
मन मनहीं समाई ।

akath kaahaani premki kachhu kahi na jaayi,
gunge keri surkaraa baithe muskaayi.
vomi bina wor beej bin thurbur ek vayi
ananth phal prakasiya guru diyaa bathaayi.
mun thir weise bichariyaa Raamhi lyo laayi
jhhuthhi mun mein visthari sub thhothhi baayi,
kahe Kabir sakathi kachhu naahin
guru vayaa sahaayi
aabun jaani miti gayi mun munhi samaayi.

Unutterable is the story of love
none can portray it.
If one tries, it will be like
the dumb explaining the sweetness of sugar
by no more than a mute smile.
Without land and seed grew
a tree bearing many fruits,
my *Guru* explained its import to me.
Thinking my mind was calm and steady
I meditated on Raam
but, all my effort went in vain.
Says Kabir, I could achieve nothing
till *Guru* came to my aid.
Then my mind became firm and staid
it united with the Eternal mind
and I bypassed the birth-death whirl.

NO. 66

अमरपुरी ले चलु हो सजना ।
अमरपुरी की सँकरी गलियां
अड़बड़ है चढ़ना ।
ठोकर लागी गुरज्ञान सबद की,
उधर गये झपना ।
वाहि रे अमरपुर लागि वजारिया
सौदा है करना ।
वाहि रे अमरपुर संत बसत है
दरसन है लहना ।
संत समाज सभा जँह बैठी
वाहि पुरूष अपना ।
कहत कबीर सुनो भाइ साधो
भवसागर है तरना ।

amarpuri le chalu ho sajanaa
amarpuri ki sunkari galiyaan
adbad hei chadhhnaa.
thhokar laagi guru gyaan subadki
udhar gaye jhapnaa.
waahi re amur pur laagi bajaariyaa
soudaa hei karnaa
waahi re amar pur sunth basath hei
dursan hei lahanaa.
sunth samaaj sabhaa jahaan baithhi
wohi purush apnaa
kahath Kabir suno bhaayi saadho
vubsaagar hei thurnaa.

O my Love!
do take me to that deathless land.
Uneven and narrow are its lanes
it is hard to go up there.
I recalled the Guru's words and went up
hoping to relax on reaching the goal.
Lo! the blessed land has come to sight,
O, here it is, its shops with wares
I wished to buy.
Here behold is the spot
where the saints are sitting in a circle
I have to bow before them.
And amidst the saints
is my Love sitting!
Says Kabir—I have to cross
the sea of earthly life yet!

NO. 67

बहुरि हम काहेकूं आवहिंगे ।
बिछुरे पंच तत्त की रचना
तब हम रामहिं पावहिंगे ।
पृथ्वी का गुण पानी सोस्या
पानी तेज मिलावहिंगे ।
तेज पवन मिलि पवन सबद मिलि,
येकहि गालि तवावहिंगे ।
ऐसे हम जो वेद के बिछुरे
सुननहिं माहिं समावहिंगे ।
जैसे जल हि तंरग तरंगिनि
ऐसे हम दिखलावहिंगे ।
कहे कबीर स्वामी सुख सागर
हंस हि हंस मिलावहिंगे ।

bahuri hum kaahe kuun aawahinge,
bichhure panch thuth ki rachanaa,
thub hum Raam hi paawahinge.
purthwikaa goon paani soshyaa
paani thej milaawahinge.
thej pavan mili pavan subad mili
ekahi gaali tawawahinge.
eyise hum jo ved ke bichhude
sunna hi maahi samaawahinge.
jeise jul hi tharung tharungini
eyise hum dikhlawahinge
kahe Kabir swaami sukh saagur
huns hi huns milaawahinge.

When I depart from my mortal body
made of the elements five
why shall I again come back here?
I shall mingle in my Lord, Raam.
The earth by nature seeps water in
I shall cause water to mingle in heat
and heat in air
and air in sound mingle
thus dissolving one in the other
and epitomize in one.
And so shall I
leaving the *Vedas* behind
mingle in the void,
and become one and the same with it
like the wave and the water.
All will notice that.
Says Kabir—My Lord is
the ocean of bliss and happiness
I shall cause my soul
to mingle in Him
the Eternal Supreme Soul.

NO. 68

सांई मोर बसत अगम पुरवां जहाँ ग॒मन हमार
आठ कूआँ नौ बावड़ी सोरह हैं पनिहार ।
महल घइलवा थंरकि गयल रे धन ठाढ़ी मन मार
छोट मोट डंडिया चंदन के हो छोट चार कहार ।
जाय उतरिहैं वाहि देसवा हो जहँ कोइ न हमार
ऊंची महलवा साहब के हो, लागी बिखसी बजार
पाप पुन्य दोउ बनिया हो हीरा लाल अपार ।
कहै कबीर सुन सांइया मोर या ही तो वो देस
जो गये सो बहुरे ना को कहत संदेस ।

saayin mor basath agum purwaah
jahaan gaman humaar.
aathh kuaan nau baawadi
sorah hei panihaar
mahul ghayilwaa thhurki gayal re
dhun thhaddi mun maar.
chhot mot dandiyaa chandun kei ho
chhot chaar kahaar.
jaay uthari hei waahi desh waa ho
jaahan koyi na humaar.
unchi mahalwaa saahab kei ho
laagi bikhasi bazar.
paap punya dou baniyaa ho
hiraa laal aapaar.
kahe Kabir suun saayinyaa mor
yaa hi tho woh desh.
jo gaye so bahure naa
ko kahath sundes.

The Lord, my Spouse
lives in that unknown unseen land
where I have to go.
Eight wells and nine land masses
and sixteen water suppliers are there.
I feel awed, benumbed and aghast
as I cannot climb up so high.
Four short and stout Sandal-wood poles,
and four bearers I arranged
and I did exhort to them—
"do carry me to the land of bliss
where I have none I know.
My Lord lives there in a towering mansion
rising above an amazing market place
where piety and sin are the two dealers
with stocks of precious diamond and gems."
Says Kabir—O my friends!
that is the land of bliss
those who go there never come back
who can portray what it is like?

NO. 69

सुतल रहलु मैं नींद भरि हो पिया दिहलै जगाय ।
चरन कंवल कै अंजना हो नैना ले लूं लगाय
जासौं निंदिया न आवै हो नाहिन तन अलसाय ।
पिया के बचन प्रेम सागर हो चलूं चली हो नहाय
जनम जनम के पापवां छिन में डारन धोबाय ।
यहि तन के जग दीप कियो प्रीति बतिया लगाय
पांच तत्त के तेल चुआये ब्रह्म अगिनि जगाय ।
प्रेम पियाला पिआयि कै हो पिया पिया बौराय
विरह अगिनि तन तलफै हो जिया कुछ न सुहाय ।
ऊंच अटारिया चढ़ि बैठलूं हो जहां काल न जाय
कहै कबीर बिचारिकै हो जम देख डराय ।

suthal rahalu mein nind vari ho
piyaa dihalei jagaay
charan kambul ke anjun ho
neinaa lelun laggay.
jaa so nindiyaan na aawe ho
naahin thun alasaay.
piyaa ke vachan prem saagur ho
chalun chali ho nahaay.
janum janum ki paapwaan
chhin mein daarub dhobaay.
yahi thun ke jug deep kiyo
preeth bathiyaan lagaay.
paanch thath ke thel chuaaye
bramh agini jagaay.
prem piyaala piyaayi ke ho
piyaa piyaa bairaay.
biruh agini thun thulfe ho
jiya kachhu na suhaay.
unch ataariya chaddhi baithlun ho
jahan kaal na jaay.
kahe Kabir vichaarike ho
jum dekh daraay.

I was in deep slumber
when my Love woke me up.
I collected the dust of His feet
and put it in my eye as *anjan*
to hinder sleep and indolence.
The words of my Love
did flow like the love tide
and formed a precious lake.
Let us have a dip there
and wash our sins of many lives.
I shall make my body the lamp
add the wick of love
and the elements five as perfumed oil,
then generate the spiritual fire
and light the lamp with it.
I have drunk from the cup of love
like mad I am shouting Love! O my Love!
the fire of yearning for my Love
is consuming me
I am in constant agony.
In ecstasy I went up the steps
of my Love's lofty mansion
where death has no access.
Says Kabir—now the King
of death is dreading my very sight!

NO. 70

तन मन धन बाजी लागी हो
चौपड़ खेल पीव से रे तन मन बाजी लगाया ।
हारी तो पिय की भई रे जीती तो पिय मोर हो
मनसा वाचा करमणा कोइ प्रीति निबाहो और हो ।
चौसरिया के खेल में रे जुग्म मिलन की आस
नर्द अकेली रह गई रे नहिं जीवन की आस हो ।
चारि वरन घर एक है रे भांति भांति के लोग
लख चौरासी भरमत भरमत पौ पै अटकी आय
जो अब कै पौ ना पड़ी रे फिर चौरासी जाय हो ।
कहें कबीर धर्मदास से जीती बाजी मत हार
अब के सुरत चढ़ाय दे रे सुहागिन नार हो ।

tun mun dhun baaji laagi ho
choupad khel peeb se re
tun mun baaji lagaayaa.
haari tho piya ki vayi re
jithi tho piya mor ho.
munsaa bachaa kurmanaa koyi
preethi nibaaho owr ho!
chousariaa ke khel mein re
jugma milun ki aash.
nard akeli raha gayi re
nahi jibun ki aash ho!
chaari varun ghur ek hai re
bhaanthi bhaanthi ke log.
lakh chouraasi bharmath bharmath
poupe atki aaye,
jo ub ke pou naa padi re
phir chouraasi jaay ho!
kahe Kabir dharmdas se re
jithi vaaji muth haar.
ub ke surath chadhaay de re
suhaagin naar ho!

I have staked my body and mind
to play dice on wager with my Love.
If I lose, my Love wins me,
If I win He becomes mine.
let others who choose
try to express their love
in word, deed, and mind.
In the game of dice
this dual hope is always there.
But, if the last draught
does not enter the home square
there will be no hope for me any more.
Same are the squares on all four sides
only the players differ.
Moving from square to square
if I cannot play the dice correctly
at the crucial stage
I shall fail to enter the home square
to reach the Lord.
And then I slide back
to repeat moving from square to square
till I come back to the home square
and enter it or slide back again.
Says Kabir to disciple Dharmadas
do not lose again and again
at the doorstep of victory
employ all your stock of love-devotion
your Love's favour to win.

NO. 71

अब घट परघट भये राम राइ
सोधि सरीरं कंचनं की नाई ।
कनक कसौटी जैसे कसि लेइ सुनारा
सोधि सरीर भयो तन सारा ।
उपजत उपजत बहुत उपाई,
मन थिर भयो तब थिति पाई ।
बाहर खोजत जनम गँवायो,
उनमना ध्यान घट पायो ।
बिन परचै तन काँच कथीरा
परचे कंचन भया कबीरा ।

ub ghut parghat vaiye Raam raayi
sodhi sarir kanchan ki naayi.
kanak kasouti jeise kasi leyi sunaaraa
sodhi sarir vayo thun saaraa
upajath upajath bohuth upaayi
mun thir vayo thub thhithi paayi.
baahaar khojut janum gumbaayaa
unmanaa dhyaan ghut paayaa.
bin parachei thun kaanch kathheeraa
parchei kanchan vayaa Kabiraa.

My Lord Raam did manifest in me,
my body now shines bright as gold!
As the goldsmith purifies gold
testing on touch-stone and treating again
so the presence of Lord Raam
purified and brightened me.
I was thinking this and planning that
but when my mind steadied
I got the clue.
Searching for Him here and there
I wasted my precious life in vain.
At length I got Him within me,
deep meditation revealed it.
Says Kabir—until the Lord did manifest
my body like glass was dull and drear
but when He did
it shone as bright as pure gold!

NO. 72

कैसे जियोगी बिरहिन पिया बिन कीजे कौन उपाय ।
दिवस न भूख रैन नहिं सुख है जैसे करि जुग जाम
खेलती फाग छांड़ि चलु सुंदरि तज चलूं धन और धाम ।
बन खंड जाय नाम लौ लावौ मिलि पिय से सुख पाय
तलफत मीन बिना जल जैसे दरसन लीजै धाय ।
बिना आकास रूप नहिं रेखा कौन मिलेगी आय
आपन पुरूष समझिले सुंदरी देखो तन निरताय ।
सबद सरूपी जीव पीव बूझो छांडो भ्रम की टेक
कहै कबीर और नहिं छूजा जुग जुग हम तुम एक ।

keise jiyogi birahin piyaa bin
kije koun upaay.
dibas na vakuh reiyen naahin sukh
hei jeise kari jug jaam
khelthi phaag chaadi chalu sundari
thuj chalu dhun wou dhaam.
bun khund jaye naam lo laawo
mili piya se sukh paay
thalputh min binaa jul jeise
darsun lijey dhaay.
Vinaa akaas rup naahin rekhaa
koun milegi aay.
aapun purus samajhile sundari
dekho tun nirthay.
subad swarupi jeeb peeb bujho
chaadon vram ki tek.
kahe Kabir wor naahin dujaa
jug jug hum thum ek.

How will you live without your Love
what means will you adopt?
Pining for Him all the time
you do not relish your food,
nor do you sleep at all
somehow you live from day to day!
Give up your playful ways, O maid
give up your wealth and abode
go to the solitude of the woods
and meditate on the Lord in peace
and tireless chant His Name.
Distraught like the fish out of water
pine and search for Him.
The Lord has no form, shape or size
come, meet Him in the void
as your dear Spouse
and never lose sight of Him.
Give up all your wrong notions
see Him as the Sound manifest.
Says Kabir—He alone is the Eternal Supreme Lord
He and I are eternally one and the same.

NO. 73

खेल ले नैहर वा दिन चार
पहिली पठौनी तीन जन आये
नौवां बाम्हन बारि ।
बाबुलजी मैं पैयां तोरी लागौं
अबकी गवन दे टारि ।
दूसरी पठौनी आप आय लेके डोलिया कहार,
धरि बहियां डोलिया बैठाइन
कौउ न लागे गौहार ।
ले डोलिया जाइ बन में उतारिन
कोइ नहिं संगी हमार ।
कहे कबीर सुनो भाइ साधो
इक घर है दस द्वार ।

khel ley naiharwa deen chaar.
pahilee pathouni theen jun aaye
novwaa bahman baari
babuljee mein payaan thori laagoun
ubki gavan deh taari.
dushri pathouni aap aaye leke doliyaa kahaar
dhari bahiyaan doliyaa baithaayin
kou na laage gouhaar
le doliyaa jaayi bun mein uthaarin
koi naahin sungi humaar
kahe Kabir suno bhaayi saadho
ik ghar hei dus dwaar.

Play for a few days in the father's house!
For taking me to my in-law's home
my Love first sent three messengers
along with *Brahmins* nine.
I fell at my father's feet
and pleaded to defer my departure.
Next my Love did Himself come
along with a *palanquin* and bearers four
He took me by my arm
and set me down in the palanquin
none raised a single word of protest.
I was carried to the deep forest
where the bearers lowered the palanquin.
None I knew did I see there.
Says Kabir—O gentle folk listen
I have only one dwelling house
with its ten doors.

NO. 74

साहब है रंगरेज चुनरी मोरी रंग डारी ।
स्याही रंग छुड़ायके रे, दियो मजीठा रंग
धोये से छूटे नहीं रे, दिन दिन होत सुरंग ।
भाव के कूंडी नेह के जल में, प्रेम रंग देई बोर
दुख देह मैल लुटाय दे रे, खूब रंगी झकझोर ।
साहब ने चुनरी रंगी रे, पीतम चतुर सुजान
सब कुछ उन पर वार दूं रे, तन मन धन और प्रान ।
कहै कबीर रंगरेज पियारे, मुझ पर हुये दयाल
सीतल चुनरो ओढ़िके रे, भइ हौ मगन निहाल ।

saaheb hei rung rej chunari mori rung daari
shyaahi rung chhudaayake re
diyo majithhaa rung.
dhoye se chhute nahi re
deen deen hoth surung.
vaab ke kundi nehake jul mein
prem rung deyi bore
dukh deha mayel lutaay de re
khhub rungi jhuk jhor.
saaheb ne chunri rungi re
peetum chatuur sujaan.
sub kucch uun pur baar dun re
thun mun dhun wor praan.
kahe Kabir rung rej piyaare
mujh pur huye dayaal
sithal chunri odhikei re
vayi ho magun nihaal.

The Lord is adept colour-expert
He has cleaned my *saari* for me.
It had become dark and ugly
and now it is bright and beautiful
in the shining colour of love.
It is no more fading from daily wash
becoming brighter day by day.
Using the water of affection
in the tub of nobleness
my Love did clean it thoroughly
and then He applied well enough
the bright soft colour of love,
my life's dirts washed away clean.
My Lord, my Love knew the art so well
I shall surrender my life, body, mind and all
at the feet of my Love.
Says Kabir—my Love the colour-expert
was so kind to me!
I shall go about now
with the cool bright *saari* on me
steeped in my Lord's love!

NO. 75

इब न रहूं माटी के घर में
इब मैं ज़ाइ मिली हरि में ।
छिन हर घर अरू झर हर टाटी
घन गरजन कांपे मेरी छाती ।
चहु दिसि बैठे चारि पहरिया
जागत मुसि गये मोरि नगरिया ।
कहे कबीर सुनहुरे लोयी
भानड़ घड़ण संवारण सोयी ।

ib na rahun maati ke ghur mein
ib mein jaayi mili hari mein.
chhin hur ghur aru jhar hur taati
ghun garajun kaampe mori chhathi.
chahudisi baithe chaari pahariyaa
jaaguth musi gaye mori nagariyaa.
kahe Kabir sunahure loyi
vanad ghadun sumbaarun soyi.

I shall no longer live in my mortal frame
I shall go and mingle in the Lord.
Feeble and fragile is my body
frail and tattered are the limbs
I shiver in panic
at the rumble of thunder.
With my mind, intellect, wisdom and ego
all intact and alert
I was robbed of all my property.
Says Kabir—O gentle folk listen!
It is God alone
who creates, protects and destroys.

NO. 76

निस दिन सालै घाव नींद आवै नाहीं
पिया मिलन की आस,
नैहर भावै नाहीं ।
खुल गये गगन किवाड़ी
मंदिर उजियारा भयो
भयो है पुरूष से भेंट
तन मन वार दयो ।

nis deen saaleh ghaaw neend aawe naahin
piyaa milun ki aash
neihur bhaawe naahin.
khul gaye gagan kiwaadi
mundir ujiyaraa vayo
vayo hei purush se bhet
thun mun baar dayo.

A sore ache pains me day and night
I do not have a wink of sleep.
I am anxious always to meet my Love,
my father's house I now dislike.
Lo! all of a sudden
the gates of Heaven opened out
and the temple of my Lord
came to view in all its splendour.
I came face to face
with my Love, the Lord Supreme
and offered my body, mind, and all
at His August feet.

NO. 77

बिरहिनी फिरै है नाथ अधीरा ।
उपजि बिना कछु समझ न परइ
बांझ न जानै पीरा ।
जा बड़ बिथा सोइ भल जानै
राम बिरह सर मारी
कैसो जानै जिनि यहु लायी
कै जिनि चोट सही री ।
संग को बिछुरी मिलन न पावै
सोच करै अरू काहे
जतन करे अरू जुगत बिचारै
रटै राम कूं चाहै ।
दीन भई बूझौ सखियन को
कोइ मोहि राम मिलावै,
दास कबीर मीन ज्यूं तलफै
मिले भले सचु पावे ।

virahini phirei hey naath adhiraa
upaji vinaa kachhu samajh na parahi
baanjh na jaanei peera.
jaa bada bethaa soyi vala jaane
Raam viraha sur maari
keiso jaanei jini eehu laayi
kei jini chot sahee ree
sung ki bichhuri milun na paawe
soch karei aru kaahei.
jathan karei aru jugath vichaare
rate Raam kun chaahei.
deen vayi bujhou sakhiyun kon
koyi mohi Raam milaawe
daas kabir min jwun thalaphe
mile valei sachu paawe.

O my Love, my Lord
for want of You, I am so distraught.
Can the childless ever feel
the pang of child birth?
Only he who has himself suffered
can understand the pang of another,
the severe pang of love.
Only my Lord who is cause of it
or who suffers the pang himself
knows its agony.
Long long ago my soul parted
from my Lord, the Soul Supreme
and now she craves re-union
but being unable is suffering
the severe pang of separation.
My soul is pining and crying always
"I want Lord Raam, my Love",
meekly my soul entreats her friends
"Can you not help me meet Lord Raam?
Says Kabir—I am suffering
like fish out of water,
I shall enjoy the bliss of Truth
if I can get my Love.

NO. 78

सो मेरे राम कबै घर आवै
ता देखि मेरे जिया सुख पावै ।
बिरह अगिनि तन दिया जराई
बिन दरसन क्यूं होइ सराई ।
निसि बासर मन रहै उदासा
जैसे चातक नीर पियासा ।
कहै कबीर अति आतुर ताई
हम को बेगि मिलो राम राई ।

so mere Raam kawe ghur aawe.
thaa dekhi mere jiya sukh paawe.
virah agini thun diyaa jaraayi
vin darsun kwun hoyi saraayi
nisi baasur mun rahei udaasaa
jeise chathak neer piyaasaa.
kahe Kabir athi athur thaayi
hum ko begi milow Raam raayi.

O my Love, my Lord Raam!
when will You come to my little hut?
my mind, and heart will fill with joy.
Separation from You
is eating me up like fire
and until I see You
it will never cool.
Like the rain-bird pining for rain
I am pining for You, my Love
and day and night I feel distraught.
I pray, I beseech you O Lord Raam
do come, do show up, do not tarry!

NO. 79

मोरि अंखियाँ जान सुजान भई
देवर भरम सुसर संग तजि करि
हरि पीव तहां गई ।
बालापन के करम हमारे
काटे जानि दई ।
बांहा पकरि करि किरपा कीन्ही
आप समीप लई ।
पानी की बूंद थै जिनि प्यंड साज्या,
ता संग अधिक कराई ।
दास कबीर पल प्रेम न घटइ,
दिन दिन प्रीत नई ।

mori aankhiyaan jaan sujaan bhayi
devar varum susar sung theji kari
hari peeb thahaan gayi.
baalaa pun kei karum humaare
kaate jaani dayi.
baahaan pakari kari kiripaa kinhi
aap sameep layi.
paani ki bund thei jini pyund saajyaa
tha sung adhik karaayi.
daas Kabir pul prem na ghatayi
deen deen prith nayi.

My eyes have gained their hallowed sight
and forsaking the company
of so-called near and dear ones
and getting over my unknowing
I have reached my Love, the Lord Supreme.
His grace has washed my life's sins
He, my Creator was merciful
took hold of me by my arm
and led me close to Him.
He, who has created me
from a drop of water
brought me close and closer to Him.
My love for Him is welling up
from day to day
and more and more anew!

NO. 80

हे बलियां कब देखूंगी तोहि
अहनिसि आतुर दरसनि कारनि ऐसा ब्यापे मोहि ।
नैन हमारे तुमकूं चाहे रती न माने हारी,
बिरह अगिनि तन अधिक जरावै ऐसी लेहु विचारी ।
सुनहुं हमारी दादि गुसांई अब जनि मारहुं वधीर
तुम्ह धीरज मैं आतुर स्वामी कांचे भांडे नीर ।
बहुत दिनन के बिछुरे माधो मन नहिं बांधे धीर
देह छतां तुम्ह मिंलहु किरपा करि आरतिबंत कबीर ।

hei valiyaan kub dekhungi thohi?
ahanisi aathur darsuni kaarani
eyesaa vyaape mohi
nein humaare thumh kuun chaahei
rathi na maanei haari.
virah agini thun adhik jaraawe
eisee lehu vichaari.
sunahun humaari daadi gusaayin
ub juni marahun vadheer.
thum dhiruj mein aathur swaami
kaanche vaande neer.
bohuth deenun kei bichhure maadho
mun naahin baandhe dhir
deha chaathaa thumh milahu kirpaa kari
aarathi bunth Kabir.

O my Love, my Lord!
when shall I see You?
Day and night I am so distraught
just to behold You
my eyes are bent on that
do not want to admit defeat.
The pang of separation pains me so
as if my body is on fire
its burning pain is too acute.
My Lord, do hear my entreaty
do not be unkind any more.
You are the very source of patience
I am a puny restless creature
unsound like the unbaked pot
that cannot hold water.
Says Kabir—O Lord, long long since
I parted from You
now my mind is too restless
for re-union
do extend Your kind hand
and take me near You
O, my Lord do hear my entreaty!

NO. 81

निबारक सुत लौ कोरा
राम मोहि मारी कलि बिस बोरा ।
उन देस जाइबो रे बाबू
देखिबो रे लोग किन किन खैवुलो ।
उड़ि काग रे उन देस जाइबा
जासु मेरो मन लागा लो ।
हाट ढूंढि ले पटन पुर ढूंढि लै
नाहिं गांव के गोरा लो ।
जल बिन हंस निहंस बिन रबू
कबीर के स्वामी
पाइ पारिकै मनै बुलो ।

nibaruk sut lo koraa
Raam mohi maari kali bish boraa.
oon desh jaayibo re baabu
dekhibo re log kin kin kheibulo.'
udi kaag re oon desh jayibaa
jaasu mero mun laagaa lo.
haat dhundi lei patun pur dhundi lei
naahin gaaon kei goraa lo.
jul vin huns nihuns vin rabu
Kabir ke swaami
paayi paarikei manei bulo.

O my Lord Raam
do pick up Your feeble son in arms.
I am harassed by the
ruinous urges of Kali
do give me your protection Lord.
O gentle folk, you have to go
to the land of my Love
and see what the people live there on
and how they live there.
O crow my friend, do fly there
where I want so much to go
visit the market places and squares
and cities and towns
and also the rural centres
and see where my Lord does stay.
I am pining for Him
like the fish out of water
I yearn for Him always
as the night's darkness
longs for the morning sun.
Says Kabir—once I get Him, my Spouse
I shall fall at His feet
and beg and win His favour.

NO. 82

मेरौ हार हिरानौ मै लजाउं, सास दुरासनि पीव डराऊं ।
हार गुह्यो मेरे राम ताग, बिचि मानिक्य एक लाग ।
रतन प्रबालै परम ज्योति, ता अंतरि अंतरि लागे मोति ।
पंच सखी मिलिहै सुजान, चलहु तजइतै तिरबेनी न्हान ।
न्हाइ धोइ कै तिलक दीन्हा, ना जानू हार किनहू लीन्ह ।
हार हिरानौ जन बिकल कीन्ह, मेरो आहि परोसनी हार लीन्ह ।
तीन लोग की जानै पीर, सब देव सिरोमनि कहै कबीर ।

merou haar hiraanou mein lajaaun.
saas duraasani peeb daraaun
haar guhyo mere raam thaag
bichi manikya ek laag.
ratun prabaalei parum jyothi
tha antari antari laage mothi.
punch sungi milihei sujaan
chalahu thaja eethhei thirbeny nhaan.
nhaayi dhoyi ke thiluk dinhaa
naa jaanu haar kinahu linhaa
haar hiraanou jana bikul kinh
mero aahi parosani haar linh.
theen log ki jaanei peer
suv dev siromani kahe Kabir.

My precious necklace is lost
I am ashamed for that
and I am dreading
my pitiless mother-in-law
and also my Spouse.
With the thread of my Lord's Name
was the necklace made
with a precious brilliant jewel as pendant
gold bits and corals
and gems of many hues in between
made it bright.
My five friends and companions
took me to bathe in *Tribeni Ghat*
there I bathed and washed me clean
they applied *thilak* to my face.
But I do not know where I lost the necklace
nor who pinched it from me.
We were all sorry for the loss of it.
I suspect my close companion
did the mischief
she stole the precious necklace.
Says Kabir—My Lord the Monarch
of all the universe
knows the sorrow of all the creatures,
And He is the Supreme God of gods!

NO. 83

अरे परदेसी पीव पिछानी ।
कहा भयो तोको समझि न परइ लागी कैसी बानी ।
भौमि बिडानी कै कहां रातो कियो काहे मोहि ।
लाहै कारनि मूल गंवावै समझावत हूं तोहि ।
निसि दिन तोहि क्यूं नींद परत है चितवत नाहिं ताहि ।
जम से वैरी सिर पर ठाडे पर हात कहाँ बिकाइ ।
झूठे परपंच में कहां लाग्यो उठि नाहिं चाली ।
कहे कबीर कछु बिलम न कीजै कौन देखी काली ।

aare purdeshi peeb pichhani.
kaahaa vayo tho ko samajhi na parayi
laagi keise baani.
voumi bidaani kei kahaan raathou
kiyo kahi mohi.
laahey kaarani mul gumwaawe
samajhaa-buth hun thohi.
nisi deen thohi quun nind parath hei
chith buth naahin thahi
jum se vairi shir per thhaade
pur haath kahaan bikaayi.
jhuthhe purpunch mein kahaan laagyo
uthee naahin chaali
kahe Kabir kachhu bilum na kijey
koun dekhhi kaali.

O alien soul wake up
do recognise your Love, the Supreme Soul
How is it you know Him not?
What has kept your senses clouded?
In unknown lands with aliens
you keep yourself tied up.
Hoping for gain you will lose your base
do take heed of my words.
Day and night you remain asleep
forgetting the Lord Supreme.
Beware death is standing guard
do not get tied to bonds of earth
do shun them this now and at once.
Says Kabir—O gentle soul do hurry
none can be sure of the morrow.

NO. 84

तोर हीरा हिरायलवा काचड़ में
कोई ढूंढे पूरब
कोई ढूंढे पछिम
कोई ढूंढे पानी पथर में ।
दास कबीर ये हीरा को परखै
बांध लिहलै जियरा के अंचरा में ।

thor heeraa hiraayalwaa kichad mein.
koyi dhunde purab koyi dhunde pachchim
koyi dhunde paanee pathhar mein.
das Kabir ye hiraa ko parakhey
baandh lihalei jyaraa ke ancharaa mein.

Your diamond is lost
in the heap of rubbish.
All search for it
some in the east
others in the west
still others in the water
or among the stones.
None get it
but Kabir the slave of the Lord
came upon and identified it
he picked it up and wrapped carefully
in the folds of his warm heart.

NO. 85

नैहर से जियरा फाट रे ।
नैहर नगरी जिन के बिजड़ी, उस का क्या घर बाट रे ।
तनिक जियरवा मोर न लागे, तन मन बहुत उचाट रे ।
या नगरी में लख दरवाजा, बिच समुंदर घाट रे ।
केसोके पार उतरि है सजनी, अगम पंथ का घाट रे ।
अजब तरह का बना तंबूरा, तार लागै मन मात रे ।
खूंटी टूटी तार बिलगाना, कोउ न पूछत बात रे ।
हंस हंस पूछों मातु पिता सों, मोरे सासुर जाव रे ।
जो चाहे सो वोही करिहै, पत्र वाही के हाथ रे ।
न्हाय धोय दुल्हिन होय बैठी, जो है पिय की बाट रे ।
तनिक घूंघटवा दिखाओ सखीरी, आज सोहाग की रात रे ।
कहे कबीर सुनो भाइ साधो, पिया मिलन की आस रे ।
भोर होत बंदे याद करोगे नींद न आवे खाट रे ।

neihur se jiyaraa phaat re
neihur nagari jinke bijadi
uskaa kyaa ghur baat re
thanik jiyarwa mor na laagei
tun mun bohuth uchaat re
yaa nagari mein lakh darwaajaa
bich samunder ghaat're
kesou ke paar utharihey sujani
agum punthh kaa ghaat re
ajab tharaah kaa banaa thamburaa
thaar laage mun maath re.
khuti tuti thaar bilagaanaa
kou na puchhatha baath re
huns huns puchhou maathu pithaa soun
morei saasur jaab re
jo chahei so wohi karihei
puth waahi ke haathh re
nhaay dohye dulhin hoye baithhi
jo hei piya ke baat re
thanik ghunghatwaa dikhaawa sakhiri
aaj sohaag ki raath re
kahe Kabir suno bhaai saadho
piyaa milun ki aash re
bhor hoth bunde yaad karoge
ninda na aawey khaat re.

She does not like her father's house.
For one distraught with that
the open road is same as home!
She longs now for the Love's house
her body and mind are agog for Him.
The city of the Lord has myriad gates
but a vast ocean is in between.
To land on the shore of the Lord
one has to cross the troubled waters.
The body is like the *Tambura*
with strings intact it sings so sweet
if the strings are snapped
none looks at it.
She told her parents gleefully
"I long to go to my Love's home."
They got enraged and retorted
"You think your Love's letter is in your hands
so you want to do as you like."
She did not heed their words,
bathed and washed herself clean
and sat down like the bride to be
to watch and wait for her Love to come.
She asked her friends—
"do lift my veil a little, dear
for tonight I wed the Lord."
Says Kabir—listen O, gentle soul!
tonight I crave union with my Love
in the morn do look me up
to see if I did not spend a wakeful night
in the bed as slave to my Love.

NO. 86

सांई बिन दरद करेजे होय ।
दिन नाहिं चैन रात नाहिं निंदिया
कासे कहूं दुख होय ।
आधी रतिया पिछले पहरवा
सांई बिना तरस रहि सोय ।
कहत कबीर सुनो भाइ प्यारे
सांई मिले सुख होय ।

saayin bin durd kareje hoye
deen naahin chayen raath naahin nindiyaa
kaa se kahun dukh hoye.
aadhi rathiyaa pichhle paharwaa
saayin binaa tharas rahi soye,
kahath Kabir suno vaayi pyaare
saayin mile sukh hoye.

My heart is aching for want of my Love.
Who shall I tell of my great distress
that I am distraught during day
and wakeful all night long?
Without my Love the whole of the night
I remain sleepless in agony.
Says Kabir—O my friend listen
I shall feel happy
only if I get my Love.

NO. 87

कोइ प्रेम की पेंग झुलावै ।
भुज के खंभे और प्रेम के रस से
तन मन आज झुलावे रे ।
नैनन बादर की झर लावै
स्याम घटा उर छाव रे ।
आवत आवत श्रुति की राह पर
फिकर पिया को सुनाव रे ।
कहत कबीर सुनो भाइ साधो
पिया की ध्यान चित लाव रे ।

koyi prem ki peng jhulaawe
bhuj ke khambe wor prem ke rus se
thun mun aaj jhulaawe re.
nainun baadur ki jhar laawe
shyaam ghataa uur chhaw re.
aawath aawath shruthi ki raah per
phiker piyaa kou sunaaw re.
kahath Kabir suno vaai saadho
piyaa ki dhyaan chith laaw re.

Do fix the swing of love today
with the arms of my Love as the poles
and His love for me as the rope.
I shall with my body and mind
swing today in this swing of love.
I shall draw from the gathering clouds
the stream of tears to my eyes
and with their lowering dark shadow
cover my heart up.
I shall bring my face close to His
and whisper in His ears
the yearning of my heart.
Says Kabir—O gentle soul listen
I shall meditate my Love in my heart.

NO. 88

सांई के संग सासुर आई ।
संग न रही स्वाद ना जान्यौ
गयो जोबन सुपने की नाई ।
सखी सहेली मंगल गावै
सुख दुख माथे हलदी चढ़ाई ।
भयो विवाह चली बिन दूलह
बाट जात समझि समझाई ।
कहै कबीर हम गौने जैबे,
तरब कंत ले तूर बजाई ।

saayin ke sung saasur aayi
sung naa rahi swaad naa jaanyo
gayo jobun supene ki naayi
sakhi saheli mangul gaawe
sukh dukh maathe huldi chaddhaayi
vayi vibaah chali vin dulah
baat jaath samajh samajhaayi
kahe Kabir hum goune jeiwe
thrub kunth le thur bajaayi.

I went with my Love to His home
But could not live with Him there
nor taste Him as my Spouse
and my youth was passing like a dream.
On the wedding day
my friends sang the wedding song
and on my head they put
the unguent of turmeric.
Thus was my wedding done
in the absence of the groom.
The wedding ended
I left with my friends,
they consoled me on the way.
Says Kabir—I shall go again
to my Spouse's home
and come back in triumph
sounding the trumpet along with Him.

NO. 89

कोटिन भानु चंद्र तारागन
छत्र की छाँह रहाई ।
मन मैं मन नैनन में नैना
मन नैना इक हो जाई ।
सुरत सोहागिन मिलन पिया को
तन की तपन बुझाई ।
कहे कबीर मिले प्रेम पूरा ।
पिता में सूरत मिलाई ।

kotin vaanu chandra thaara gan
chhathra ki chhaanha rahaayi.
mun mein mun neinun mein neinaa
mun nainaa eek ho jaayi.
surath sohaagin milun piyaa ko
thun ke thapan bujhaayi.
kahe Kabir mile prem puraa
peethaa mein surath milaayi.

Under the canopy of my Lord
millions of sun, moon and stars do shine.
Would to Him His mind in mine,
His eyes in mine unite
and both think and see alike.
And if I could unite with Him as His beloved
the heat of my body would vanish.
Says Kabir—if I too could get His love
I would link my face to His
and drink with Him from the same cup of love.

NO. 90

गली तो चारो बंद पड़ी म्हारे पियासों मिलन कैसे होय ।
काम क्रोध लोभ मद मोह ने घेरी चारों गैल ।
इन गलियन में मेरे प्रीतम बसते कैसे करुं मैं बाकी सैल ।
पांच पचीस पहरवा ठाढे रोक लिये सब ठाम ।
यह विधान ने कैसे कीनी बैरी बसाये म्हारे गांम ।
आसा तृष्णा खड़ी दुहेली इन में रहा समाय ।
कनक कामिनी गहरा फंदा अंत तजो नहिं जाय ।
ग्यान भक्ति बैराग जोग का मारग दियो बताय ।
कहे कबीर सुनो भाइ साधो बिन प्रेम ना कोई आये ना जाय ।

gali tho chyaaro bund padee
mhaare piyaa se milun keise hoy?
kaam krodh lov mada moha ne
gheri chyaaro gayel
in galeiyun mein mere prethum vasathey
keise karuun mein waa ki sayel?
paanch pachees paharwaa thhaade
rok liyea sub thhaam
yaha bidhaan ne keise keenee
bairee basaay mhaare gaam.
aashaa thrisnaa khadee duheli
in mein rahaa samaay.
kanuk kaamini gaharaa phundaa
unth thajo naahin jaay.
gyaan vakthi vairaag jog kaa
maarug diyo vathaay.
kahe Kabir suno bhaayi saadho
bin prem naa koyi aawe naa jaay.

All the four lanes are fully blocked
how can I go and meet my Love?
Lust and anger, greed and pride
have encompassed these lanes
where my Love does stay.
How can I go to meet Him there?
All these lanes are strongly guarded
by the five and twenty guards,
with all their men and arms
they have covered all the lanes.
Besides, the foes who live always in me,
the longings and urges of the earth
the mighty lures of lust and lucre
all so hard to discard
they add to the barrier.
To surmount them
I have been told to follow the paths
of knowledge, devotion and penance.
Says Kabir—O gentle folk listen!
none can enter the lanes nor emerge
who does not know the way of love!

NO. 91

राम बिना संसार धंध कुहेरा सिर प्रगट्या जम का पेरा ।
देव पूजि पूजि हिंदू मुये तुरक मुये हज जायी ।
जटा बांधि जोगी मुये इन मे किनहु न पायी ।
कवि कबीन कविता मूये कापड़ी के दारौ जायी ।
केस लुंचि लुंचि मूये बरतिया इनमें किनहु न पायी ।
धन संचते राजा मुये अरू ले कंचन भारी ।
वेद पढ़ें पढ़ि पंडित मुये रूप भूले मुई नारी ।
जे नर जोग जुगति करि जानै खोजे आप सरीरा ।
तिनकूं मूकति का संसा नाहीं कहत जुलाह कबीरा ।

Raam binaa sunsaar dhanddh kuheraa
shir pragatayaa jum kaa peraa.
dev puji puji Hindu muye
thurak muye huz jaayi
jataa baandhi jogi muye
in mein kinahum na paayi
kavi kavin kavitha muye
kaapdi kei daaroun jaayi
kesh lumchi lumchi muye varathiyaa
in mein kinahum na paayi.
dhun sanchathe raja muye
aru le kunchan vaari
ved padhen padhhi pundhith muye
rup vule muyee naari.
je nur jog jugathi kari jaane
khojei aap sariraa
thinaku mukathi ki sansaa naahin
kahath julaah Kabiraa.

Without Lord Raam
life is hollow and unreal
like fog or smoke.
Men remember not
death is ever standing guard
with his relentless crusher in hand.
The Hindu worships his deities and dies
the Muslim goes on huz and dies
the saint grows matted hair and dies
but none of them ever realise the Lord.
The poet dies writing his poems
the pilgrim visiting sacred places
the austere ascetic
painfully pulling out his hair
they too do not realise God.
The king hoards his gold and dies
the pundit reads his scriptures and dies
the woman bedecks her body and dies
but none of them realise Him.
Says Kabir—only he who knows the way of love
and seeks Him with the inward eye
within his own self
doubtless he will unite with the Lord
and achieve salvation.

NO. 92

खसम न चीन्है बावरी
का करत बड़ाई ।
बातन लगन न होयेंगे
छोड़ो चतुराई ।
साखी सबद संदेस पढ़ि
मत भूलौ भाई ।
सार प्रेम कछु और है
खोजा सो पाई ।

khasum na chinhey baavari
kaa karath badaayi.
bathan lagan na hoyenge
chhodo chathuraayi
saakhi subad sundesh padhhi
muth bhulo bhaayi
saar prem kachhu wor hey
khojaa so paayi.

Man, you know not your own Lord yet
what are you so proud of?
Your cleverness will be of no avail
mere words will not help you
to unite with the Lord.
Do not be deceived
by the scriptures, songs, and messages
true love is something else.
He only knows
who sought it with a steadfast heart.

NO. 93

राम बान उन्यालै तीर
जाहि लागै सो जानै पीर ।
तन मन खोजौं चोट न पाऊं
औषध मूली कहां घसि लगाऊं ।
एकहि रूप दिसै सब नारी ।
ना जानै को पियहि पियारी ।
कहे कबीर जा मस्तिक भाग
ना जानूं काहु देइ सुहाग ।

Raam baan unyaalei theer
jaahi laage so jaanei peer.
tun mun khojoun chot na paaun
ousad muli kahaan ghasi lagaaun.
ekahi roop disei sub naari
naa jaanou ko piyahi piyaaree
kahe Kabir jaa mustik vaag
naa jaanu kaahu deyi suhaag.

The Name of Lord Raam
is like a sharp, unfailing arrow
he knows the pang of it
whom it ever hit,
but in your body or mind
no wound you find
where shall you apply the remedy?
Women appear all alike
who knows the one beloved of the Lord?
Says Kabir—none knows the lucky one
on whom the Lord
will give His mark of love!

NO. 94

राम बिन तन की ताप न जाई
जल मे अगिनि उठी अधिकाई ।
तुम्ह जलनिधि मैं जलकर मीना
जल में रही जलही बिन पीना ।
तुम्ह पिंजरा मे सुवना तोरा
दरसन देहु भाग बड़ मोरा ।
तुम्ह सतगुरू मैं नौतम चेला
कहै कबीर राम रंमु अकेला ।

Raam bin thun ki thaap na jaayi
jul mein agani uthhi adhikaayi.
thuma jalanidhi mein jalakar minaa
jul mein rahi jul see vin peenaa.
thumh pinjaraa mein suvanaa thoraa
darasun dehu bhaag bade moraa.
thum sathguru mein nouthum chelaa
kahe Kabir Raam ramum akelaa.

Without you, Lord Raam
the heat of my body will not abate
it will wax inspite of a dip in water.
O Lord! you are like the vast ocean
I am a little fry in it
but I do not drink a drop of the water.
You are the cage
I am Your parrot in it
but I cannot see Your face at all.
Says Kabir—O Lord, You are the true preceptor
and I am Your fledgeling disciple
only with Your mercy, my Lord
can I see Your face
and remain united with You.

NO. 95

जो मैं बौरा तो राम तोरा
लोग मरम का जानैं मोरा ।
मैं बौरी मेरे राम भरतार
ता कारन रचि करौं स्यंगार ।
माला तिलक पहरि मन माना
लोगनि राम खिलौना जाना ।
थोरी भगति बहुत अहंकारा
ऐसे भगता मिलै अपारा ।
लोग कहैं कबीर बौराना
कबीर का मरम राम भल जाना ।

jou mein bouraa tho Raam thoraa
log marum kaa jaane moraa.
mein bouri mere Raam vurthaar
thaa kaarani rachi karun syangaar.
mala thilak pahari mun maanaa
logani Raam khilounaa jaanaa.
thhori vagathi bohuth anhankaaraa
eise bhagataa melei apaaraa
log kahei Kabir bouranaa
Kabir kaa marum Raam bhal jaanaa.

If I am mad Lord, it is for You!
others have not any scent of it.
Lord Raam is my Spouse
I am mad for Him
and for Him alone I bedeck myself.
People treat Him as a toy
think their *thilak* mark
and *thulsi* necklace are enough.
Scant devotion and plenty pride
such devotees everywhere you find.
People say, Kabir is mad
but Lord Raam knows Kabir too well.

NO. 96

मेरे तन मन लागी चोट सठौरी
बिसरे ग्यान बुधि सब नाठी
भइ बिकल मति बौरी ।
देह बिदेह गलित गुण तीन्यूं
चलत अचल भइ ठौरी ।
इत उत जित कित द्वादस चितवत
यहु भइ गुपत ठगौरी ।
सोइ पै जानै पीर हमारी
जिहि सरीर यहु धौरी ।
जन कबीर ठग्यौ है बापुरै
सुनि समानी त्यौरी ।

mere thun mun laagi chot sathhouri.
visare gyaan buddhi sub naathhi
vai vikal mathi bouri.
deha bideha galitha guna thinyu
chaluth achal vayi thhouri.
itha utha jith kith dwadus chitha batha
yuhu vayi gupath thhagouri.
soyi pei jaanei peer humaari
jihi sarir yahu dhouri.
jana Kabir thhagyo hei baapurei
suni samaani thyouri.

The pang of my love
for the Lord has caused
an acute ache in my body and mind.
All my senses and intellect
are dulled and inactive.
I am feeling so distraught and restless
my limbs are benumbed sans sense of feeling
I am not able to walk two steps
as though for me the world of the Gunas
is non-existent.
And Lo! as if by secret magic
I behold in all directions
the effulgence of twelve suns!
Only I know the maddening pang
of the love of the Lord
and he knows who himself has suffered.
Says Kabir—all my senses
are now centred in the void
where the Lord does manifest.

NO. 97

आस नहिं पूरिया रे राम बिन को करम काटन हार ।
जब सर जल परिपूरिता चात्रिग चित हि उदास
मेरी विसम करमगति ह्वै परि ताते पियास पियास ।
सिध गिलै सुधि ना मिलै मिलावै सोई
सूर सिध जब भेंटिये तब दुख न ब्यापै कोई ।
बौछे जलि जैसे मछिका उदर न भरई नीर
त्यूं तुम्ह कारनि केसवा जन ताला वेलि कबीर ।

aas naahin puriyaa re
Raam vin ko karam kaatanhaar
jub sur jul paripurithaa
chaathrig chithahi udaas.
meri bisum karam gathi whe pari
thathe piyaas piyaas.
sidhh mileh sudhi naa mileh
milaawe soyi
sur sidhh jub vetiyea
thub dukh na byaapei koyi.
bouchhei juli jeise machhikaa
udar na varayi neer
thyun thumh kaarani kesavaa
jana thaalaa veli Kabir.

My hope is not yet fulfilled Lord Raam!
who save you can mitigate
all my life's misdeeds?
When the reservoir is full
the night-bird is cold and callous.
I am harassed by the outcome
of all my life's misdeeds
and I am so distraught.
Many so called sages have I met
but none has given the clue to me
only if I meet the real saint
then my suffering will abate.
Says Kabir—like the fish dying of thirst
though always living in water,
for want of Lord Raam
I am in great distress.

NO. 98

करो जतन सखि सांइ मिलन की ।
गुड़िया गुड़वा सुपलिया
तजिदे बुधि लरिकेया खेलन की ।
देवता पितर भुइंया भवानी
यह मारग चौरासी चलन की ।
ऊंचा महल अजब रंग बंगला
सांइ की सेज वहां लगि फूलन की ।
तन मन धन सब अरपन कर वहाँ
सुरत सम्हार परूं पइयां सजन की ।
कहै कबीर निर्भय होय हंसा
कुंजी बता द्यों ताला खुलन की ।

karo jathun sakhi saayin milan ki
gudiyaa gudwah supaliyaa
thajide budhi larikeyaa khelan ki
debata pithar bhuyaan vabaani
yaha maarag chouraasi chalan ki.
uncha mahul ajub rung bunglaa
saayinki sej waahaan laagi phulan ki.
thun mun dhun sub arpan kar wahaan
surath sumhaar paruun payaan saajun ki.
kahe Kabir nirvay hoy hunsaa
kunji vatha duon thaalaa khulun ki.

O my friend strive your best
for union with the Lord.
Give up now the childhood
habits of playfulness.
If you invoke the temple gods and goddesses
and spirits of the ancestors
that will be of no avail
for your salvation.
In yonder bright and lofty mansion
is laid the bed of the Lord
bedecked with flowers of many hues.
At His feet surrender yourself
body, mind and all.
Says Kabir—O gentle swan!
proceed without fear and faltering
use the key that I have given
to open the lock.

NO. 99

हमने इस्क मस्ताना हम को होसियारी क्या
रहे आजाद या जग सौं हमन दुनिया से प्यारी क्या ।
जो बिछुड़े हैं पियारे से भटकते दर बदर फिरते
हमारा यार है हममें हमन को इंतजारी क्या ।
खलक सब नाम अपने को बहुत कर सिर पटकता है
हमन हरि नाम राचा है हमन दुनिया से यारि क्या ।
न पल बिछुड़े पिया हम से न हम बिछुड़े पियारे से
उन्हीं से नेह लगा है हमनं को बेकरारी क्या ।
कबीरा इस्क का माता दुई को दूर कर दिल से
जो चलना राह नाजुक है हमन सर बोझ भारी क्या ।

humne isk musthaana
humn ko hosiyaari kyaa?
rahe aajaad yaa jugsoun
humn duniyaa se pyaari kyaa ?
jo bichhude hein piyaare se
bhatak the dur badur phirthe,
humaaraa yaar hei hum mein
humnko inthajaari kyaa?
khaluk sub naam apne kou
bohuth kur shir patak thaa hei.
humn hari naam raanchaa hei
humn duniyaa se yaari kyaa?
na pul bichhure piyaa hum sein
na hum bichhure piyaare se
unnhi sei neha lagaa hei
hum ne ko bekaraari kyaa?
Kabiraa isk ka maathaa
duyi ko dur kur dil se
jo chalnaa raaha naajuk hei
humn sur bojh vaari kyaa?

I am drunk with the love of the Lord
why should I be care-worn?
I am free from the ties of the world
no love for it have I any more.
Separating from my Love I am
wandering here and there.
But lo! my Love does stay in me
I have not to seek nor wait for Him!
All are self-centred on earth
they beat their heads and hands
but I am always chanting the Lord's name
I have not to befriend the world at all.
I shall not again separate from the Lord
nor allow Him to leave me alone.
He is my Lord, my only Love
why should I be distraught?
Says Kabir—I am now fully drunk
with the love potion of the Lord
and banished all my doubts of mind
why should I worry any more?
When the road is narrow and hurdlesome
why should I carry a heavy load?

NO. 100

प्रीति लागी तुम नाम की पल बिसरे नाहीं
नजर करो अब मेहर की मोहि मिलो गुसांई ।
विरह सतावै हाय अब जिया तड़पै मेरा
तुम देखन को चाह है, प्रभु मिलो सवेरा ।
नैना तरसे दरस को पल पलक न लागै
दरद बंद दीदार का निसि बासर जागै ।
जो अबके प्रीतम मिलै करूं निमिस न न्यारा
अब कबीर गुरू पाइया मिला प्राण पियारा ।

preethi laagi thum naam ki
pul bisre naahin.
najar karo ub mehur ki
mohi milo gusaayin.
virah suthaawe haay ub
jiya thadhpei meraa
thum dekhun ko chaao hei
pravu milo suberaa.
nainaa tharase darus ko
pul paluk na laagey
durd bund didaar kaa
nisi basur jaagey.
jo ubkei prithum mile
karun nimis na nyaaraa
ub Kabir guru paayiyaa
milaa praan piyaaraa.

I am in love with Your Name my Lord
I do not forget it for a moment.
Do shower Your grace on Your slave
and let him behold You.
I am so distraught for want of You
the pain of it is too acute.
With all my heart I want You my Lord
do come soon.
My eyes so yearn to see Your face
winkless they gaze
wakeful all day and night
for a glimpse of You.
Says Kabir—when I get my Lord, my Love
I shall not for a moment
lose sight of Him
He is my Love, my preceptor, my eternal Lord!

NO. 101

सरवरि तटि हंसिनी तिसाई
जुगति बिना हरि जल पिया न जाई ।
पिया चाहै तो ले खग सारी
उड़ि न सकै दोउ पर भारी ।
कुंभ लिये ठाढ़ी पनिहारी,
गुण बिन नीर भरै कैसे नारी ।
कहै कबीर गुर एक सुधि बताइ
सहज सुभाइ मिलै राम राइ ।

sarbur thati hunsini thisaayı.
jugathi vinaa hari jul piyaa na jaayi.
piyaa chaahei thou leh khug saari
uddi na sakei dou para vaari.
kumbha liye thhaaddi panihaari
gun bin neer varey keise naari.
kahe Kabir guru ek sudhi bathayi
sahuj suvaayi mile Raam raayi.

Standing at the pool
of the Lord's Nectar
the swan is going thirsty!
She does not know how to drink the Nectar.
Without the know-how
none can drink of it my dear!
Both her wings are too heavy
not knowing how to, she cannot fly.
With pot in hand the maid is standing
but without the rope
she cannot draw water from the well
to fill her pot.
Says Kabir—my *Guru* gave me the clue,
by following simple innocent habits
I can realise Lord Raam.

GLOSSARY OF NON-ENGLISH WORDS AND OBSCURE EXPRESSIONS USED

No. 1	elements five	- Namely earth, water, air, heat, and void of which the human body is composed.
	Brahma	- The first member of the divine trinity Brahma, Bisnu, and Maheswar who manage the universes under the unseen impulse of the Supreme Formless God who is in eternal samadhi (meditation) according to Kabir's conception of God-Head.
	Vedas	- The original scriptures of Sanatan dharma which initially existed in words of mouth.
No. 7	all the five	- Refers to the five well known enemies of man namely lust, ire, pride, worldly attachment and jealousy.
No. 8	consort's mark	- Refers to the practice of the bridegroom putting the vermilion mark on the bride's forehead signifying their marriage.
No. 9	swan	- The saints have used the term 'swan' for the human soul after its release from the body on death. Kabir has made extensive use of this term in his songs and Dohas.
No. 11	Ganges and Yamuna	- Signifying the two principal nerves, 'ida' and 'pingala', respectively, lying on the left and right side of the spinal cord in the human body—this has much to do with Hata Yoga.
No. 12	night bird	- The little bird bearing the name "chakor" or chakua is known to be too fond of gazing at the moon winklessly.

No. 13	saari	– The bordered cloth usually coloured or printed, used by the Indian women as their ordinary wear. Kabir has used this term or "Chunri" or "Chaddar" symbolically to mean the human body.
No. 15	scaring the crow	– In parts of rural India women still believe in the crow indicating the future by partaking from little heaps of paddy, rice, or wheat for which the bird is scared to come at the heaps again and again.
No. 18	Fakir	– Literally a wandering mendicant of Islamic faith—here Kabir refers to the Lord.
No. 20	rain bird	– A little bird of lark variety called 'Papiha'. It is said she drinks only the rain drop water and not any other water.
	swati-rain	– Rainfall when the swati star is in the sky.
No. 25	parrot	– Life bird or breath of life.
No. 27	celestial drum	– Refers to the cosmic music (anhad) which is permeating the entire universe and said to be holding everything together, by charm as it were.
No. 33	on the Ganges on the Yamuna	– Vide note under item 11.
	five farm workers	– Refers to the five sense organs, eye, ear, nose, tongue and skin.
	seven grains	– Skin, blood, flesh, fat, bone, marrow and semen.
No. 35	dark night	– Refers to death.
No. 42	Diamond	– Refers to the Lord.
No. 45	elements five	– See notes under No. 1.
	aarati	– The ritual of offering lighted candles during worship of the God.

No. 46	Gem	- Refers to the Lord.
No. 55	father's home	- Refers to the earthly home where man is born.
	five palanquin bearers	- The five sense organs vide notes under No. 33.
No. 57	Brahmin	- Means the priest who dresses the dead body with new clothes before cremation as is the practice in parts of India.
No. 60	*saari*	- The human body vide notes under No. 13.
	stains	- The evil effects of the five permanent enemies of man viz lust, ire, greed, attachment and pride showing in the words, thoughts and actions of men.
	washerman	- Helper.
	applied turmeric	- As a form of auspicious anointing at the time of marriage.
No. 61	Five constant friends	Are the five sense enemies, lust, ire, greed, attachment and pride. They have been sarcastically called friends as they do not leave man even till his death.
No. 65	without land and seed	- Many fruits—symbolically express that God who is father of all the creation, Himself has no creator. He created Himself.
No. 66	but I have to cross the sea of life yet	- Kabir presents an imaginative mental picture of God before actually meeting Him.
No. 67	elements five	- Vide notes under No. 1.
No. 69	*anjan*	- Also called *kaajar*, a dark sticky preparation for anointing the eye.
	elements five	- Vide notes under No. 1.
No. 70	dice	- An indoor game of ancient origin played by four persons, two to a side. Sometimes it is played on wager. Was popular with kings and monarchs of ancient times.

No. 81	Kali	– The last of the four Ages (Satya, Treta, Dwaper and Kali) according to Hindu conception, and current now, full of sin and strife.
No. 82	Tribeni ghat	– The confluence of three sacred rivers Ganges, Yamuna and Saraswati believed to be the most sacred confluence. A dip there washes away all sins, people believe.
	thilak	– Composition of silt of sacred rivers dyed in different colours for different religious sects for putting their distinctive marks on forehead, arm etc.
	five friends and companions	– The five enemies of man such as lust, ire, greed etc., sarcastically called friends and companions.
	constant companion	– Greed.
No. 85	Tambura	– Old version of modern Tanpura, a stringed musical instrument.
No. 86	Canopy of my Lord	– The sky.
No. 90	five and twenty guards	– The five enemies of man viz lust, ire, greed etc., each with his four allies.
	four lanes	– Symbolically the four main veins which join the heart and arteries for passage of blood from and to the heart. The heart is believed to be the abode of the Lord vide last five lines of the song.
No. 93	mark of love	– The vermilion mark put by the bridegroom on the forehead of the bride.
No. 95	*thulsi*	– An Indian herb believed to have been in her life one of the beloveds of Lord Krishna, one of the *Avatars* of the Supreme Lord.

No. 96 Gunas	- The three 'gunas' of 'Satwa', 'Rajas' and 'Tamas' meaning truth, animality, and untruth. Men are said to belong to one or other of these three categories by nature.
No. 101 Guru	- Preceptor of Hindu faith.

37. My mind do dance in delight _____ 78
38. It is indeed hard to win the Lord _____ 79
39. With my friends and companions _____ 81
40. O gentle lady, why do you not wash your blouse _____ 83
41. Evening shadows darken deep _____ 84
42. When my mind overflows with love _____ 85
43. My eyes are drooping with sleep, my Love _____ 86
44. Nectar rained down from the sky _____ 87
45. Soaked is the body and mind of the beloved _____ 88
46. Maiden, do wake up from your slumber _____ 89
47. O Love, do come this once inside my eye _____ 90
48. O my friend for want of my Love _____ 91
49. I am not able to come to You _____ 93
50. The Lord is my Love, O friend _____ 94
51. O gentle folk, why are you groping in the dark? _____ 95
52. I do not relish my stay with parents _____ 97
53. If you cannot win the love of the Lord _____ 98
54. O my friend let us go there _____ 99
55. My Lord arranged a palanquin _____ 100
56. I am out in search of my Love _____ 101
57. My Love had brought me the farewell saari _____ 103
58. O my Eternal Love, Protector of devotees _____ 105
59. Watching always for my Lord _____ 106
60. In my saari did I sustain stains in my father's house 107
61. My Love is awake, how can I sleep? _____ 109
62. O Raam, my Love, for many and many a day _____ 111
63. I went to my father-in-law's house to be near my Spouse _____ 113
64. I bedecked myself for meeting my Love _____ 114
65. Unutterable is the story of love _____ 115
66. O my Love, do take me to that deathless land _____ 117
67. When I depart from my mortal body _____ 119
68. The Lord, my Spouse lives in that unknown unseen land _____ 121
69. I was in deep slumber when my Love woke me up 123
70. I have staked my body and mind _____ 125
71. My Lord Raam did manifest in me _____ 127
72. How will you live without your Love _____ 129
73. Play for a few days in the father's house _____ 131
74. The Lord is adept colour expert _____ 133
75. I shall no longer live in my mortal frame _____ 134
76. A sore ache pains me day and night _____ 135
77. O my Love, my Lord for want of You, I am so distraught _____ 137
78. O my Love, my Lord Raam _____ 138

79. My eyes have gained their hallowed sight _____ 139
80. O my Love, my Lord, when shall I see You _____ 141
81. O my Lord Raam do pick up your feeble son
    in arms_____ 143
82. My precious necklace is lost, I am ashamed for that 145
83. O alien soul wake up, do recognise your Love, the
    Supreme Soul _____ 146
84. Your diamond is lost in the heap of rubbish_____ 147
85. She does not like her father's house _____ 149
86. My heart is aching for want of my Love _____ 150
87. Do fix the swing of Love today _____ 151
88. I went with my Love to His house _____ 152
89. Under the canopy of my Lord, millions of sun, moon
    and stars do shine _____ 153
90. All the four lanes are fully blocked _____ 155
91. Without Lord Raam life is hollow and unreal _____ 157
92. Man, you know not your own Lord yet _____ 158
93. The Name of Lord Raam is like a sharp unfailing
    arrow _____ 159
94. Without you, Lord Raam, the heat of my body will not
    abate _____ 160
95. If I am mad Lord, it is for You_____ 161
96. The pang of my love for the Lord has caused_____ 163
97. My hope is not yet fulfilled Lord Raam_____ 164
98. O my friend strive your best for union with
    the Lord_____ 165
99. I am drunk with the love of the Lord_____ 167
100. I am in love with Your Name my Lord _____ 168
101. Standing at the pool of the Lord's Nectar _____ 169

BC/14-1-13/10 (0033)